WHY HE BETRAYED JESUS

VIKTOR SHEL

Copyright © 2016 by Viktor Shel
All rights reserved.
No part of this publication may be reproduced,
stored in a retrieval system, or transmitted,
in any form or by any means, electronic, mechanical,
photocopying, recording, or otherwise,
without the written prior permission of the publisher.

ISBN: 978-9890856-6-3

Editor: Cathy Reed.

Cover Design: Iryna Spica.
Typeset at SpicaBookDesign in *Plantin*.

Printed and bound with www.createspace.com.

Preface

DESCRIBING THE LIFE of Judas Iscariot, this book proposes a position directly opposite to the common narrative. From the depths of the Middle Ages, we have been told that Judas was a despicable traitor, and his name has become a symbol of betrayal in many languages.

But was it so? Was it a deliberate act of betrayal of Jesus for monetary gain, or was it a necessary decision, orchestrated by Jesus himself, with the purpose of establishing a new religion, not only for Jews but for other peoples on this earth?

Imagine if Judas had been just one of the twelve loved disciples of Jesus, and that Jesus, surrounded by his small group of devoted followers, had continued to wander about in Judea until his old age, preaching to curious listeners whose numbers sometimes grew and sometimes waned. In that case, there would have been no further development of Judaism and we would not have such a religion as Christianity. Judas had to help with arrest of Jesus to ignite process of creation of the new religion.

The emergence of Christianity required establishing the foundation for a new religion. The *martyrdom* of Jesus, whom followers recognized as the Son of God, created this foundation. Jesus suffered for the sake of mankind – and created a new religion. The genius of Jesus was that he realized the need for such a sacrifice, and HE organized it.

Jesus consistently acted to anger the priests of the temple in Jerusalem and the ruling Jewish elite to make them wishing his death. For this, he publicly declared himself the messiah and a descendant of King David.

What's more, there is no doubt that it was he who sent Judas to the High Priest to arrange for his arrest. Judas was an actor, a performer in the play that Jesus had conceived; and this also explains the death of Judas very soon after he had fulfilled his task.

Contents

Preface v

1   Meeting With Jesus. 1
2   Honor Earthly and Celestial 19
3   The Reflections of Judas. 47
4   The High Priest Kiafa 62
5   The Affairs of Jesus 74
6   Jerusalem 89
7   The Last Supper. 103
8   Fulfillment of Destiny. 115
9   Hello Eternity! 129

About the Author 141
List of Published Works. 143

One
Meeting With Jesus

YOUNG JUDAS ISCARIOT wandered long after his parents' death, but nowhere could he find refuge and nowhere could he find peace. Every night he would wake up terrified by his frightening dreams. Most often, he dreamt that he was lying on his back in the middle of the city square, which was in front of his parents' house, and that the Roman legionaries around him were ruthlessly killing people. All of the square was strewn with corpses and severed heads and gutted bellies. The blood rushed to the leaves of the shrubs, to the walls of the houses, and to the earth. Even the sky was a pink color as if it had been painted with blood.

Against this background, a Roman legionary towered above him with a terrible smile. With one hand he raised his sword above Judas' head, and with the other, he pointed his knife at Judas' stomach. And blood poured out everywhere. This vision had come to Judas every night since that terrible day, never allowing him any peace.

The events that Judas had experienced in his hometown were what caused his dreams. The residents of the town had rebelled against the new tax imposed by Rome, and as punishment, a Roman legion surrounded the city and slaughtered its inhabitants, including Judas' father and mother. Judas survived due to his ability to run like the wind. He broke through the chain of legionaries and ran out of town to the mountains where he hid in a cave. He stayed there for several days, afraid to leave the cave, but hunger and thirst finally drove him out of the shelter.

Judas returned to his town. The city had been completely destroyed by the legionnaires, and the corpses of residents lay everywhere, poisoning the air with the suffocating odor of decay. Flocks of black birds fell on the bodies of men, women and children, and Judas averted his eyes from the unimaginable horror.

When he went to the house of his parents, he found the corpse of his mother on the doorstep, split into pieces with a sword. Nearby lay his father, the insides of his stomach spread out on the road. The scene was so horrifying that Judas fled from his native town, never to return. What he had seen pursued him everywhere he went, and his soul knew no rest day or night.

Judas walked to where his feet carried him, having no notion of where he should be going. People in the villages that he passed would, on rare occasions, give him food, but more often they chased him with dogs and sticks. Judas struggled to survive by way of the rare alms he was given and by hard labor wherever he could find it.

In one village, he lingered for six months. A villager was building a stone house and he needed an assistant. The local limestone was harvested close by in the mountains. Using primitive tools, the laborers chipped the mountain stone into large chunks and then hewed them into the necessary shape required by the builders.

The owner hired Judas to work on shaping the stones and the work was hard and tedious. Judas would hit the stone all day long, trying to create the required shape. At first, he found it very difficult, but eventually he learned to do the shaping quickly and well. Unfortunately for Judas, the work ended when the owner had accumulated enough hewn stones for the construction. Judas then had to leave the village and go further in search of work; during his six months of hard labor, he had earned only the food he ate and the mat on which he slept at night.

For several years Judas wandered, always looking for work and shelter. He did not find a place where he could settle permanently; even finding a place for a short stay was sometimes difficult. After years of wandering in Judea, his legs led him to Galilee. The residents of this region did not hurry to shelter the stranger, despite the fact that they lived a wealthier life than that of the people in the mountains of Judea. They looked on Judas as a foreigner, even though they spoke the same language and prayed from the same book; and Judas rarely managed to find a job, even as a day laborer. He kept walking along the road, often finding food in the bushes, which in Galilee grew in abundance.

Judas was feeling lonely and in despair, when on the road he met a small group of pilgrims who were as poor as he was. The pilgrims were kind and friendly, and those unfortunate and hungry men shared with Judas the crumbs of food that they had. One pilgrim told Judas that they were traveling to Galilee to listen to a man named Jesus, a prophet. They had heard many rumors about him as they were travelling.

"Who is this famous prophet?" Judas asked.

"People tell all sorts of stories about him. They say that he cures incurable diseases, and that he teaches by word and deed. And they say that his teaching is so wise that even well known Pharisees cannot argue with him.

"Apparently, some of the experts regarding the Holy Books given to us by God are surprised by his knowledge and his conviction. They do not understand how this son of a simple carpenter could study the books so deeply that no one can point to any errors in his knowledge. So we would like to hear him, to ensure that the rumors do not deceive us. If it turns out that what has been rumored about him is true, then we would like him to transmit to us at least a small part of his holiness."

Judas was surprised by these kind people and their desire to walk such a distance just to listen to an intelligent man. Judas, without any plans for his future, and not knowing what to do next, decided that he would like to listen to this man and perhaps ask for his advice. Maybe he would find in his sermons something what would comfort his lacerated soul. The good prophet might be able to tell him where to put his energy and how to live in the future. So Judas joined the group of pilgrims.

The rumors about the places where Jesus preached gradually led the group to Gennesaret Lake. It was the first time that Judas had seen this famous lake that was as broad as the sea. The waves of the lake made a soothing noise that calmed Judas, and a gentle breeze cooled his body and soul.

Near the shore, in the shadow of the spreading trees, they found a group of people listening attentively to a lean man who spoke with feeling and conviction. One of the listeners whispered to Judas: "That is Jesus!"

Jesus was dressed modestly. His face was thin and his eyes shone. The words flowed from his lips gently and confidently. Mesmerized by his sermon, the audience listened carefully to every word of the preacher, trying to understand the meaning of what he was teaching.

Judas loved Jesus at first sight, not only because Jesus spoke so convincingly, but because Jesus radiated kindness, which Judas had been so deprived of since the death of his parents. The soul of Judas reached out for kindness, like a sunflower opening to the sun.

Jesus fed the people who came to listen to him with barley bread, and Judas devoured the bread like a hungry beast. He had not eaten bread for a very long time, living mostly on a lean broth of leaves and lentils. After eating, Judas listened with great attention to the preaching of Jesus, and every word of the prophet settled in the depths of his soul.

To the group of people who were listening to Jesus came a nobleman from Capernaum and he was taken to Jesus.

"Rabbi," the courtier said, "my son is ill, and nobody has been able to cure him. He is so bad that death is near. Would you have mercy on me and go to my house to heal my only son. I believe in you and I ask you to go quickly before it is too late. You are the one hope I have left."

"Do not be sad, good man," Jesus replied with a soft, firm voice. "God is merciful. Go home safely; your son is cured."

The courtier could scarcely believe the words of the prophet, but when he looked at the calm face and the kind eyes of Jesus, he believed what Jesus had said, and he turned homeward.

Judas heard the words of Jesus and he could not believe that his words had healed the nobleman's son. Such confidence seemed impossible! But not long afterward, the courtier's servant came and said that the boy was miraculously cured. It was indeed a miracle.

After the miracle he had witnessed, Judas believed in Jesus, and he vowed to follow him wherever he went and learn from him, if Jesus would allow him to do so.

So Judas followed the prophet, listening to his every word and watching his every gesture and every act. And Jesus noticed the eagerness with which Judas heeded his teachings. Jesus liked Judas, and this was noticed by the other companions of Jesus.

They went from village to village, carefully listening to the teachings of Jesus when he spoke to the people. Many of those who followed Jesus paid careful attention to his words and endeavored to understand the meaning of his sermons and parables. Judas remembered the words of the Prophet better than most and their meaning gradually became clearer to him. Jesus noticed that Judas was not only diligent but also quick-witted.

They travelled from village to village, and in each village, Jesus enlightened his disciples and all those who wished to listen to him. People came from many different places, having heard about the incendiary sermons of Jesus. But in one village, very few people came to listen to the preaching of Jesus, and one of the men explained that some of his fellow villagers had gone to a nearby village to listen to the preaching of another preacher by the name of Reuben. Hearing this explanation, Jesus asked Judas to go to the village and listen to what Reuben was saying. Judas reluctantly agreed.

Judas arrived in the middle of the sermon and joined the group of listeners. Reuben, an old man with a white beard, was dressed in white ashen dust clothes and spoke passionately about the importance of the commandment 'Thou shalt not kill!' In the opinion of Reuben, the commandment should relate only to not killing Jews.

"This commandment does not apply when referring to those who do not believe in the only God, the

Creator;" said Reuben. "These people oppress the people of Judah and do not hesitate to kill the Jews, and for this reason, this commandment should *not* apply to them. To confirm his words, he gave an example from the book "Numbers" of the conquest of the land by Jesus the son of Joshua. Jesus, blessed by the Creator himself, killed some of the inhabitants of Canaan, freeing the cities and the land for the Chosen People.

Judas realized that the preaching of Reuben exhorted the people of Judah to fight and he justified rebellion in the name of God. Reuben made a bad impression on Judas. It was not just his speech, but rather to the anger and hatred that radiated from his preaching. Although Judas himself had reason to hate the Romans because they had deprived him of his parents in a horrific manner, the heart of Judas under the influence of Jesus had softened, and he was open to love and rather than hate. But Reuben, bursting with anger, fervently preached vengeance. Judas did not like being around him.

Jesus listened attentively to Judas's report on the preaching of Reuben, and he said: "A preacher should never inspire people to hate. A preacher's goal is to teach people the truth about the true God, the Creator of all things on earth. All people on earth are His creation and He loves every person. The Romans just did not know Him, and as little children they were taught to worship other gods."

After this, Jesus went into a period of meditation so he could think about how to bring all the people on earth to believe in the Creator, his Father.

After he had meditated, Jesus realized it was time to choose twelve trusted disciples and teach them to preach and to perform miracles. Among others, Jesus chose Judas Iscariot as his aide and apostle. This choice surprised many because all the apostles were from Galilee—only Judas was from Judea. People asked one another: "How do you explain that Jesus chose one from Judea? What in this young man attracted the attention of the prophet? Perhaps Jesus did not find among the Galileans enough young men worthy of learning?"

"We do not know the answer," the apostles replied. "Our Prophet likes people of all lands ... from Galilee, Samaria ... so why can't he choose as his apostle a young man from Judea? He seems to like him."

However, the apostles did not count Judas as equal to the others. He had no wife, no home; he was an itinerant laborer doing odd jobs. A poor wanderer was no match for hard working fishermen.

But slowly Judas found his place in the group. Some of the apostles believed that his sincerity came from stupidity, and his greed for knowledge they explained as the desire to curry favor with Jesus. One thing was clear to all: the young man was ridiculously naive and honest, although terrified to death by the pogrom of his native village and the death of his parents. Jesus knew about the death of Judas' parents and he successfully helped the young man to recover somewhat from his fear of the future. Gradually Judas retrieved some of the happiness that had been characteristic of his youth. In place of his parents, Judas now had Jesus as a teacher and mentor.

The group had a box in which they put the money that was given to them by generous listeners. The box was heavy and awkward to carry. Because they travelled on foot and had no animals to carry their belongings, no one wanted to take the box in addition to their personal belongings. The disciples decided that the young Judas was strong enough to carry the box of cash, and that he could cope with this additional burden even on the long passages. Along with this box, the duty of treasurer went to Judas, and Jesus endorsed the decision of the apostles.

Judas took his new duty of treasurer seriously, and he tried to save every copper coin for the community. When he purchased produce for the group, he always bargained, and when he received cash offerings, he carefully counted them, always ready to report on the state of the register.

Some in the group appreciated his diligence, but there were those who liked to make fun of him, jokingly accusing him of taking money from the register. Judas reacted nervously and was very offended by the false charges, thereby encouraging more pranks. Usually the pranks were kindly, and when Judas understood that it was a joke, he calmed down and did not take offense. He even came to understand that the jokes and fun were a necessary part of long passages from village to village.

As well, some of the apostles loved to entertain with jokes during the long passages in their journey, and Judas was sometimes the target of their jokes. Jesus generally didn't mind the friendly banter, as long as the jokes did not interfere with his thoughts, but there were cases when Jesus asked the apostles to calm down and not disturb his thinking.

In his sermons, Jesus inspired the disciples by explaining his divine origin as the reason for the success of the miracles that occurred. He taught his disciples that only God can create miracles, and that God works miracles through the people who believe in him. Gradually, the students took over the art of preaching and it gladdened the heart of the teacher. Jesus had high hopes for his best disciples like Peter, John and Judas. There were cases when Jesus was busy preaching in one village and sent his disciples to give a sermon in another village.

Although the disciples looked on Judas with a certain amount of distrust, the women of the community were friendly and kind to him. Mary Magdalene had a special sympathy for Judas, the early-orphaned youth. She accepted him almost as a son, making sure that Judas was always fed and cared for. Being the closest to Jesus, Mary saw that Jesus trusted Judas and appreciated how carefully he treated the community property. Judas responded to the kindness of Jesus and Mary with respect and filial love. Mary was happy to see that Judas was gradually able to get rid of his fear of choking. She drew attention to the fact that Judas' feelings of fear had been replaced by boundless faith in Jesus and His mission to educate people.

In the months that Judas was in the community, he learned quickly. For him, studying was easier than for the others, because he was very young and because he was more educated than the fishermen. When his parents had been alive, they had paid a great deal of attention to educating their son. Judas had read all five books of Moses; had learned to speak, read and write Greek; and he could freely express himself in Latin. Among the other apostles, who were fishermen, only Peter and John were able to speak Greek. Jesus wanted to spread the belief in one God, the Creator of the Universe, among all peoples on Earth; and therefore, he appreciated the foreign language skills of his disciples.

A test of faith in Jesus was the case in Jerusalem where Jesus healed a crippled man one Saturday when Jesus and his disciples went as a group to the temple to pray. At the Sheep-Pool, there is a place with five colonnades; its name is Bethesda. At this place, the group saw many poor and sick people who sought to bathe in the pool, which had five layers. The people believed that the first individuals who entered the pool on Saturday would be healed from illness. The lame, paralyzed, blind and deaf jostled to experience the life-giving water. At the entrance, a crippled man was lying on his bed and looking plaintively at the crowd of people.

The men from the group accompanying Jesus saw him and one of them explained:

"This man for thirty-eight years has been lying on his bed, unable to get up and get into the pool. How can he possibly be among the first to reach the water when there are many sick people jostling at the entrance and interfering with each other to reach the water first?"

"He lies there for that long?" Jesus asked. "Apparently he believes deeply in the healing properties of the water."

Jesus stood at the bedside of this man and asked, "Do you want to recover?"

"My Lord! Of course I wish to recover, but there is no one to put me in the pool when the water is distributed. There is always someone in the pool before me."

"Rise to your feet, and take your bed and walk," Jesus said to the sick man.

The man recovered instantly, took up his stretcher, and began to walk. Everyone around him was astonished. The recovered man wanted to bow at the feet of his healer. He looked around but could not see the one who had healed him. Jesus had slipped away in the crowd.

Distressed, the healed man walked with his bed to find Jesus. The deeply religious people saw him and they attacked healed man: "It is the Sabbath. How dare you carry your bed on the holy Sabbath? God has commanded that thou shall not perform any work on the Sabbath!"

The elderly man responded: "The man who healed me said: 'Take your bed and walk.' I am grateful to him and I want to thank him!"

"Who is the man who told you to take your bed and walk?"

"I do not know him, but I think he is a saint, and it is a sin to disobey a saint. I want to worship at his feet and I am trying to find him."

Jesus' disciples heard this conversation and some of them wondered why Jesus had asked the man to carry his bed. That evening, they talked about it. They discussed whether or not it was a sin to carry one's bed on the Sabbath.

"The Sabbath is the day of rest. One should not carry anything that day!" Simon the Zealot said. "If we stopped observing the Sabbath, we would become pagans like the Romans."

"You're probably right, friend Simon," Thomas confirmed.

Judas was upset that his friends dared to discuss Jesus' order. "You're both wrong," he said. "Jesus, our teacher, is a holy man. Whatever he commands must be fulfilled exactly."

The next morning, they went to the temple to pray. Jesus saw the crippled man who had been cured and he recognized him. The man recognized Jesus too.

"Thank you for curing me!" he said, bowing low to the prophet.

The believers surrounded the healed man, asking: "This man told you to carry your bed on the Sabbath?"

"Yes, he did! He is a holy man!" The healed man exclaimed.

"What sort of saint is he, if he ordered you to violate the Holy Sabbath?" the deeply religious people asked.

"How dare you heal on the Sabbath!" exclaimed one of the faithful, shouting at Jesus. "Get out of the temple!"

Jesus looked at him with regret, and said: "My Father has never ceased his work, and I am also doing his work. The Son can do nothing by himself; through me, the Heavenly Father is doing his work. If He works wonders on the Sabbath, then so be it. As the Father raises the dead and gives them life, so the

Son gives life to men. I am always doing just what my Father tells me to do! Who honors my Father shall honor me because my Father sent me and gave me jurisdiction! As I hear, I judge: and my judgment is righteous, because I do not judge by my whim, but by the will of my Father who sent me."

The disciples and believers looked respectfully at Jesus. Such miracles indeed could only be performed by the Creator, and who but the Lord knows best what is permitted to do on the Sabbath and what is not?

That evening the disciples argued about whether or not the claim of Jesus that he was the Son of God could be justified. They knew that there was a carpenter in Nazareth named Joseph and that Jesus was his son. Because of this, some believed that Jesus' statement should not be taken literally. They believed that Jesus was just a spiritual son of the Lord. They were convinced that the Spirit of God moved into the soul of the carpenter's son. It was only at this point that Jesus was the Son of God.

Judas never doubted the word of Jesus. He took Jesus' word literally, believing that Joseph was the father who brought up Jesus, but the Lord himself was the real father of Jesus, exactly as Jesus claimed. He was sure that if the Teacher said he was the Son of God, then it was undoubtedly so. A Holy man is Holy because he always tells the truth. Judas expressed his thoughts aloud, and Peter agreed with the argument of Judas.

"Of course he is the Son of God," Peter said. "How would the Teacher accomplish wonders if he is not given the strength of the Lord? Only to his son does God give such abilities."

Judas was grateful to Peter for supporting him in such an important matter. However, some of the other apostles did not agree with Peter, referring to the fact that Jesus of Nazareth had a father, a simple man who did not have the gift to do miracles. They concluded that Jesus was himself an amazing miracle and therefore should be considered as the Son of the Creator, because it was impossible to perform miracles without the support of the Lord, the Creator of the earth and everything on earth.

The disciples were leaving Jerusalem confident that between Jesus and the Lord God there was a connection, perhaps the same as between father and son. The consciousness of this communication attracted the disciples and gave them hope that through Jesus, some of God's grace would be passed on to them. They did not know how heavy was the burden that they voluntarily took upon themselves. Following the path of Jesus, many of them were destined to meet the same fate as Jesus. Their path was thorny, but they would be remembered and respected by people for many centuries. Only one of them would be doomed to undeserved eternal shame.

Two
Honor Earthly and Celestial

SEVERAL MONTHS LATER, Jesus was walking along the rocky road deep in thought. His closest disciples walked some distance behind, not wanting to bother the Teacher. After the disciples ran the boys, and at the end of the procession the women walked along in a group. The blazing sun heated the boulders of the surrounding hills like stove tiles, further warming the already hot air. It was hard to breathe and even harder to climb up the hill by a barely noticeable path that Jesus of Nazareth had chosen.

Judas Iscariot was the last in the group of disciples, and this was no wonder because he was loaded like a pack donkey. In a huge knapsack tied behind Judas' back were a mat for sleeping, a sheepskin sack of water, a cauldron and, most importantly, the storage box for donations, in which jingled the coins of different values. Peter and John were laden only with their mats. They were the favorite pupils and they used this to their advantage.

The group reached the top of the hill and started to descend into a cozy valley. Among fields sown with barley were the visible roofs of the village, located in the center of the valley. The olive trees surrounding the village were well cared for and their branches were dark with fruit. At the entrance to the valley, the road was devoid of vegetation and skirted by high rock.

Jesus stopped, turned to his disciples, and said: "Let us stay there, in the shadow of the rock. I must think."

"Teacher," John said, "Is not it better to get to the village and spend the night under a hospitable roof?"

"I am not keeping anyone here," Jesus said. "Whoever wants to stay in the village is free to go to the village. I am staying here. Walls confine me. I need a spacious and clean sky for rest and reflection."

"Our teacher is right," Peter said. "We are in Judea and not in Galilee. The men of Judea are not always friendly to us. They are dark; their souls are not open to the righteous words of the Teacher. They may not accept us."

"Let us go to the shadow side of the rock," Jacob said. "I'm hungry. Hey, Judas, unfold your knapsack and take out the pot. I will stack stones for the fire."

The students scattered among the rocks in search of brushwood for a fire, and the women settled not far away. The boys ran to the village, shouting: "The Prophet has come! A descendant of King David is with us! Wise words he tells! He works wonders!"

"Do not shout; I'm not deaf!" answered the peasant working in the field near his home. "Many people pass by here! All beggars declare themselves prophets!"

From the house came a lame old man leading a blind teenage boy by the hand. "What wonders?" the old man asked the boys.

"He has cured people from all misfortunes!" one of the boys explained. "Bow to him; ask him to heal your grandson."

"Why not bow? What do we risk? My grandson is blind; he has not seen the light for a long time. If there be no cure, so we have no luck, but if your prophet can cure him, it will be a miracle and it means your teacher is a true prophet!"

"Father, do not be naïve," the farmer said to the old man. "So many charlatans walk by, and you ask all of them to heal the boy, and so far no help."

"Father," the young man said. "I will go with my grandfather. Grandfather is right; I have nothing to lose. I cannot see anything, but I feel in my heart that this prophet is real. I believe in this prophet! He will do a miracle!"

"If he asks for money in advance, do not give him any," The father said to his son. "Go with God."

The farmer went into the house. He did not believe the boys. He was used to the fact that through the village, standing on the road to Jerusalem, pilgrims walked to the Temple. Many of them, in order to support themselves, indulged in quackery, convincing naive peasants that they could work miracles. Typically, their spells lead to nowhere. It was true that this time the prophet came with a large group of people, but this could only mean that he was a skilled charlatan and knew how to fool people. The farmer did not believe in wandering preachers.

Meanwhile, at the foot of the boulder, the disciples had built a fire and cooked a pottage. Judas lay exhausted on his mat, placing the cash drawer under his head. Even though he was young and strong, he was very tired and he desperately wanted to sleep.

In the group of disciples, he was not the most popular. The majority of them were fishermen from the Sea of Galilee, and they did not trust Judas, who came from Judea. Judas himself was somewhat wary of the other disciples; their childish fun sometimes irritated him, and he did not like the fact that they often didn't understand the preaching of the Master. It was true that some of the Teacher's parables at first seemed incomprehensible, but after clarification Judas always understood the hidden meaning. The others, even after hearing the explanation, did not necessarily understand simply taking the words of Jesus as a revelation.

For example, Jesus told the parable of the sower:

A sower went out to sow;

And when he sowed, some seeds fell along the footpath; and the birds came and ate them up.

Other seeds fell on rocky ground where there was a little soil, and they sprouted quickly because they had no depth of earth;

When the sun rose, the young corn was scorched, and because it had no roots, it withered away;

And some of the seeds fell among thistles, and the thistles grew up and choked the corn;

And others fell into good soil, where they bore fruit, some an hundredfold, some sixtyfold, some thirtyfold,

If you have ears, then hear.

Matthew 13:4,9

Judas did not understand what this parable meant. None of the disciples understood and they came to Jesus to ask its meaning. Jesus explained that only the elect are given the ability to know the mysteries of the kingdom of Heaven, but this is not given to all. As the prophecy of Isaiah states: "You may listen and listen, but never hear; you may look and look but never see."

And Judas understood that those who had hardened their soul would not see the kingdom of Heaven; that only true believers, not burdened by sin, would enter the kingdom of Heaven. Jesus was a great Teacher and it was a great honor to Judas to learn from such a wise and holy man. Many times Jesus reproached those who considered themselves superior to others. Even his parables spoke about the need to respect the weak. Therefore, Judas did not pay attention to the fact that the fishermen treated him contemptuously. He listened to the Teacher and rejoiced in the knowledge he acquired.

Jesus sat on a smooth rock that faced toward Jerusalem. He silently thought about the upcoming Easter holiday celebration of the miraculous rescue of the Jews—who believed in one God—from slavery in Egypt. Jesus, like all deeply religious Jews in those days, planned to pray in the Temple of Jerusalem on this holiday. The Temple would bring him closer to his Heavenly Father. Jesus, the son of Joseph the carpenter of Nazareth, believed in his heart that he actually had two fathers—one who conceived him and one who brought him up. Joseph brought him up, but God, the Creator of the Universe, had conceived him. All his life he had wanted to meet his Heavenly Father eye to eye, but he only saw him in dreams, in visions. In these visions, Jesus consulted with his Father, the Creator, and he received instructions.

Jesus was sad, and sometimes resentment burned his soul. How was it that a Father could hold his son for so long away from himself? Really, why could he not see his Heavenly Father on this holiday? Jesus knew that he was a Child of Man, and like all individuals born by a woman, his soul was trapped in a human body. Only by freeing his soul from corruptible flesh would he be able to join his Father.

Why did his Father not free him from this human shell? What were his Father's plans? Upon giving birth to an earthly Son, the Father should have planned something. What had He planned? Jesus was convinced that the plans of the Creator included the belief in only one God for all men living, regardless of their ethnic origin. Yes, He had created the Chosen People. He had loaded this nation with strict rules and prohibitions, and it was difficult to comply with all His requirements. Only the Chosen People had this ability, and the number of Chosen People was small; a drop in the human sea. His Father was probably hurt, knowing that only the small nation of Judah honored His name. He certainly wanted all peoples on Earth to believe in Him. But it was difficult for all the diverse peoples of the world to observe all the prohibitions. The rules and prohibitions should be simplified so that even the most ignorant people in the world could observe them.

Jesus believed that there was a need for a world religion, where everyone living in the world would believe in one God, the Creator of the Universe. Jesus passionately wished for people to believe in not only his Father, but the Son of God also. In this new World Religion perhaps not all the bans would be met, but it was important that the key moral and ethical rules become the rules of all humankind. Was not this the purpose of the Father? If not for this purpose, why did the Father conceive him? The problem for Jesus was how to create a religion for all mankind. What kind of ideas would attract *all* people?

Jesus believed in His Father's goal, but he did not know how, from the simple and accessible sermons that he so skillfully preached, a new World Religion would be born? He needed something that would appeal to the mind of all people and lead them to faith in the one and only God.

Jesus thought about this problem, not being able to convey his thoughts to his disciples. All of them, his disciples and followers, were not sufficiently developed and educated to the point where he could trust them with such an important matter as the creation of a World Religion. Only Judas, coming from a wealthy and educated family was literate enough to understand the purpose and the objectives of the Father. But Jesus felt that Judas was not destined to carry his Father's problem; Judas had another mission. Who else? Jesus had only the apostles he had selected; He would work with them.

Jesus knew that, for the apostles to be able to start a new religion. He would need to come with some new critical ideas that were capable of attracting all peoples. If Jesus did not endow the minds of the apostles with such an idea, they would not be ready to perform what they were destined to do, and the Father would not allow Jesus to join Him.

Jesus decided that the purpose of the day's lesson was to explain the fear of death and the existence of the soul of each person. The most primitive human instinct is the fear of death. This feeling is present in all living things, and it is impossible to get rid of it. All people are mortal, and only immortality can suppress the fear of death. Immortality it is not meaningless for people because there is an immortal soul in each person. How could He instill in the minds of these fishermen that the flesh is not the whole man. The body lives for a short period of time but the Universe exists eternally. Although the body is mortal and will perish, there is within the mortal body, as if in a prison, an immortal soul, and this is the essence of the person.

The soul, freed from its prison, will not die. At that point, it begins an independent eternal life.

Jesus called to His disciples. They surrounded Him, lying down on their mats in a semicircle. After the dinner and the long journey through the Judean Desert, they wanted to rest, but their strict teacher called them and they reluctantly prepared to listen to Him. Only one of them, Judas, who took a place in the second row, was ready to listen to his beloved Teacher with pleasure.

"Listen to me, my pupils! I bring you near to Himself with the aim to give you the knowledge and skills that you will require. We spoke about the human soul that is destined to come closer to God; only the blessed souls will live forever in Paradise. Blessed are those who follow the teachings. The exercise that I bring to you is a basic moral rule: "Do not do to others what you would not like them to do to you." This is the cornerstone, but it is the most difficult to comply with. Everyone wants to imagine a better lot and is ready to fight for it; but in this fight, one does not notice that he is seeking his share at the expense of others. He makes them do what he would not want them to do to him, and this violates the great commandment. Violators of the commandment cannot be blessed. Is that clear?"

Andrew turned to Jesus. "Rabbi, you're talking about the soul? Is the soul responsible for the actions of the body? The body is hungry; it requires food. And food can only be obtained by taking from another person. So the soul will plead: "Do not take," but the body will snatch a piece of food from another anyway, because the body does not wish to die."

"That man has a weak character who allows the body to control his soul," Jesus said. "Do not be afraid of death; be afraid of violating the covenants. Every one of you must not break the covenant, and you must teach this to others. Just by the example of your own behavior, you can convince others to observe the law."

"Rabbi, what kind of law are you talking about? Do you mean the law of the ruling Romans?" Simon the Zealot asked.

"We do not fight with the rulers, but we care primarily about compliance with the laws of God," Jesus replied calmly.

Noises came from the road, and Judas saw an old man with a young boy trying to get to their group, but the women were not allowing them.

"What is all that noise about on the road?" Jesus asked. "Judas, go and find out."

Tired Judas did not wait for the Teacher to repeat the request. He quickly got up and went to the women. The old man, surrounded by the women, looked at Judas with pleading eyes and said: "Please, dear man, allow my grandson to go to the prophet. He asks the prophet for the mercy of healing his blindness."

Judas scratched his ear, wondering whether it was convenient to ask the Teacher when he was teaching his pupils. Judas knew that Jesus would not refuse to help the sick, but it might be better to wait for the end of the lesson. Then Judas thought how impatient he would be if he was the blind boy, if he knew that the healing hand was near. Judas could not detain the young man, knowing how difficult this delay would be for him.

Judas thought that this was the first example of a basic rule: "Do not do to others that you would not want done to you."

"Come on, boy. I hope that the teacher will help you," Judas said.

Jesus was not offended. He interrupted his teachings and listened to the young man's request.

Jesus said to the boy: "Close your eyes. Do you believe that you will recover? How deeply do you believe that God will not leave you in the lurch?"

"Rabbi, I believe that Almighty God will not refuse me. I truly believe in the power of God!" the young man said passionately, keeping his eyes closed as Jesus had commanded.

"To those who believe, healing will come," Jesus said. "Open your eyes and admire the light of day."

The young man opened his eyes and then closed them quickly and opened them again.

"Oh, great prophet! I believed in you, and you

did not disappoint my expectations!" the happy young man shouted.

"Believe in God. Your belief in the omnipotence of God saved you!" Jesus said.

The young man knelt down and said: "Blessed be Thy name forever and ever."

The young man realized that Jesus wanted to continue the lesson with his disciples, and he hurriedly left the foot of the cliff, screaming at the top of his lungs: "Blessed be your name forever and ever!"

Judas, lying on his mat, was happy for the young man. He thought: "Truly blessed be Thy name forever and ever." Jesus continued lecturing his disciples.

For Judas, it was not easy to communicate with the other disciples. When Jesus had chosen him along with eleven others as his immediate disciples, Judas was very surprised. Given that all the other disciples were from Galilee, Judas did not believe that Jesus would choose him. But Jesus noticed the young Judas and brought him to the group. Moreover, Jesus entrusted him with the public funds; this was a special duty and Judas was very proud that Jesus had trusted him.

The apostles were at first pleased that the duty of carrying the public box was given to Judas because it was heavy and awkward to carry. But when they saw how Jesus completely trusted the treasurer of the community, this caused some envy among the other followers. Judas tried not to notice that some of the disciples were somewhat hostile toward him.

The disciple Simon, whom Jesus called Peter, particularly liked to bully Judas, and he often mocked Judas to amuse the other disciples. Judas did not take offense. His reason for joining Jesus was not to make friends with his disciples; his aim was to learn from the Teacher's truth. Judas, instead of responding to Peter's sometimes offensive jokes, counted this unpleasantness as his initiation.

Judas repeatedly pondered the reason why Jesus had chosen him, knowing that Jesus did not do anything without a plan. Did this mean that the teacher planned to use Judas for something for which he could not use his disciples from Galilee? What was the difference between the people of Judea and the sons of Galilee or Samaria? It came to Judas' mind that perhaps it was a fanatical dedication; life in Judea was harder than in the fertile valleys of Samaria and Galilee because the ground of Judea was covered with rocks and it was very difficult to grow crops. The inhabitants of Judea, living in such harsh conditions, sincerely believed that only God helped them to survive. They were more fanatical in their faith than people in other parts of the country; and due to their proximity to the Jerusalem Temple, they visited the Temple more often.

The residents of Judea hated the Gentile Romans and Greeks more than any other people in the country did and they suffer from the Roman yoke more than others.

Fanaticism sometimes manifests itself in the actions of unexplained reason. Here the Roman ruler of Judea, Pontius Pilate started to build in Jerusalem plumbing system. Plumbing is very useful to the city, but it was purely a Roman innovation. From Roman stuff like plumbing business can move to a more serious change the usual way of life of the city. Give in to this useful fact, look, and harmful innovations follow. People revolted against the construction of the aqueduct. Judas joined the protesters, although he knew that the aqueduct no religious oppression would not bring. Pilate soldiers beat protesters with batons. Judas then got so that he left the city and since there did not return. He returned to his parents only to witness the terrible massacres performed by Romans.

Well here is that he joined at the Sea of Galilee the crowd listened to the sermon of Jesus. Judas believed in the teachings of Jesus with all his heart and followed him everywhere. He listened attentively to the preaching of Jesus, his parables and wondered Teachers victories over the Pharisees in disputes about the truth. Judas was the first to believe in the divine origin of Jesus.

The evening came and the whole camp went to sleep. Judas lay on his mat and admired the stars. These small lights in one part of the sky shining in the dark sky as the point at the other are grouped in the nebulas. Judas remembered how Jesus explained that each such nebula consisted of a set of stars located in a small area of the sky. Stars are so small and so close to each other that when looking at the sky, stars merge and look to the eye as a bright spot. Judas wanted to have such a keen eye to distinguish individual stars in each of the nebula. The teacher taught that each star was a celestial angel, and each such angel controlled the soul of a human on earth. Judas wondered which star was his angel?

Very early in the morning, when the sky was still lit up with stars, Jesus rose from his mat and headed up the hill. During the night, the stones of the hill cooled and were covered with moisture. Jesus chose a convenient place and sat on the cold cobbles. Now, away from the sleeping apostles, he indulged in meditation. He thought for a long time and His thoughts were about the Heavenly Father and His plans. This morning the plans of the Father became clear to Jesus. Jesus saw that the Father had put before him the task of ensuring that all people in the world believed in Him, the One God. Not only the chosen people, but all peoples would abandon their faith in many gods and come to believe in the One God. But how to attract them? How to convince the idolaters that there is only one Creator of the Universe?

It was not an easy task. How to convince those who believed in different gods, when even the Jews, who already believed in the Creator, did not want to believe in the divine origin of Jesus? Many people, after hearing him preach, began to believe in the divine origin of Jesus. But then when they went to the Temple and listened to the priests of the temple claiming that the Creator could not possibly have a son on earth from a human woman, those people began to question Jesus' claim. The very notion of the Son of God contradicted the main postulate of Judaism — that there is only one God, Creator of the Universe. How, in such conditions, to attract all people on earth to have faith in the Holy Father?

Jesus strongly believed that after the death of perishable flesh, life does not end. At the moment of the death of the body, the Soul is freed up for the continuation of life. And only the sinless soul will attain eternal bliss; a soul burdened by sins will not see bliss. Sin means that the soul will suffer eternal torment in hell.

But people have a problem because there are no innocent people. Sometimes a person commits a sin unintentionally, but even such sinners cannot see Heaven. So what to do? How to make it so that human souls can access Heaven? How to make sure that for everyone who truly believes, forgiveness of unintentional sins is possible?

Jesus believed that faith in the eternal bliss of the soul was something that could attract humanity to believe in the true God, the Creator. The problem was to find a way to ensure the salvation of souls for all humankind. This task was grand and noble, but very difficult...and perhaps unsolvable!

Jesus thought about this. Why unsolvable? There should be a way to solve this problem! Jesus looked down from the top of the hill to the sleeping valley and saw the beauty of nature. The green valley was surrounded by huge black mountain rocks as if giants were guarding the peace of the residents. Jesus thought: "What can be more beautiful than such a spectacle? All this beauty is the handiwork of my Divine Father! For my Father it was not easy to create all this beauty, but he succeeded! Am I so weak that I cannot solve the problem of how to make people believe? I must find a way of bring all peoples to faith in the Father! I will find it!"

Suddenly it dawned on Jesus that although all people are sinners, there exists a rite for clearing people of their sins. The annual animal sacrifice at the Temple is a rite to clear people of their sins over the entire year! So this type of sacrifice is the proper way to clear people's soul from their sins!

But it cannot be a simple animal sacrifice, as priests perform in the temple; it must be something much greater. What kind of sacrifice would be good enough to bring salvation to all people on the Earth? It must be a huge thing. It must be so great that it will clear all the sins of the people, and not for one year, but forever!

Who could make such a sacrifice? Someone who is responsible for all people on Earth. And who would that be? Only the Creator is responsible for everyone on Earth. So the sacrifice must come from the God himself! He must sacrifice something extremely valuable to Him. What is to the Heavenly Father so precious, so important, that being sacrificed could save all Mankind? Of course! Such a huge sacrifice would be HIS son, the only Son of God! Jesus suddenly understood that HE must be this sacrifice! He was born for this noble reason and it was His personal destiny! Only through terrible suffering and death, would He be able to bring salvation to all Mankind and join His Father in Heaven!

Jesus became frightened of his own thoughts. It was easy to say he would give himself as a sacrifice, but to do so would be very difficult. Sacrifice meant first of all suffering. How to survive the pain and anguish? Death is not a frightening thing, but the terrible pain during torture is frightening. It was frightening that he himself must give his body, his own flesh to this torture! It was terrible even to think about making such a step. Jesus pinched himself; it was painful. If a simple pinch was painful, what would torture be like? How could he withstand it?

Jesus tried to find something positive in death. What did he want? He wanted as soon as possible to join His Father. It seemed that only through the suffering and death of his human body would his soul be free for the desirable reunion with the Heavenly Father! Yes, the flesh must die first, then the Father would resurrect him and he would dwell with the Father in the kingdom of Heaven forever.

Undoubtedly, this was God's plan! It was so clear now that Jesus marveled at why he had not understood this previously.

So now that Jesus understood his Father's plan, it was time to consider how to implement it successfully. Who would bring suffering and death? The Roman pagans enjoyed making people suffer; they enjoyed watching the suffering of slaves dying from their wounds! Only the Romans could expose a person to martyrdom. However, the Romans did have laws, and they could not punish an innocent person. For a death sentence, someone would need to convince the Roman governor that by preaching in Judea, Jesus had committed a terrible crime against Rome. Who would see Jesus' actions as a crime? To whom would his preaching seem dangerous?

Only to the priests in the Temple of Jerusalem. They were afraid of the impact of the new prophet. They feared him and hated him. The Pharisees hated him too. Jesus knew that the people of Judah, to whom he preached every day, liked him and would want to defend him. Therefore, the temple guards would not arrest him when the crowds were surrounding Jesus and listening to his preaching.

They would want to arrest him at night. But at night all wolves sulfur. How would the Guards find him without the help of someone who was close to Jesus? Only one of the people close to Jesus could point him out at night in the dark. Who of the disciples would so imbued by purpose and plans of Jesus that without flinching would point at him, while not revealing the plan of Jesus to the others? This was not a simple assignment; it was associated with shame. So who? Peter? No, he was clever, but his personal ambitions would not allow him to connect his name with such a shameful business. After all, the other disciples would never understand the one who would betray Jesus. He would be cursed on the Earth forever. Only in Heaven would be known the true courage of this man.

In his mind, Jesus considered all of the apostles, and it seemed to him that only one of them was so steadfast and loyal that he would not hesitate to perform *any* mission, if Jesus instructed him to do so. That was the apostle Judas Iscariot.

Jesus thought. Judas was the apostle who was best able to attract people to the new faith. Judas knew Latin, Greek, and could easily learn other languages. Judas was a gifted orator. Actually, Jesus greatly valued Judas the apostle for his oratorical skills. To entrust to

Judas the role of the traitor meant to lose him as a missionary. Without him, it would be much more difficult to attract the crowds to the new faith. No, it was necessary to save Judas. Whom else could he entrust with this critical and unpleasant mission? Maybe Simon the Zealot? He was also fanatically devoted. He could run an errand, but only if he understood the meaning of the task. Jesus had no doubt that Simon would hide the secret from his enemies, even if it would cost him his life, but as for friends that he trusted, Simon might not be able to hide the secret. Could Jesus trust the secret of the whole plan to Simon? It would be a disaster if Simon would reveal the secret to even one of his friends, because then everybody would know it. No, Jesus could not trust the task to the boastful and frank Simon.

Whom else? Jesus turned over in his mind the advantages and disadvantages of each of his twelve apostles, and he could not find one who would be better suited than Judas Iscariot to perform this difficult and extremely unpleasant mission. Judas was the only one who would do the job and not reveal the motive of Jesus.

Jesus was terribly sorry for Judas. He was the most talented and the most faithful and loyal disciple. Yet he would be the victim. Jesus was extremely conflicted.

The sun rose and woke up the whole camp. It was a long way to the next village. John gave everyone leftover bread; Thaddeus brought a leather bag of water from the creek; and Judas went into the town to buy food. Jesus returned to the camp, took his portion of bread and washed down with water. The disciples looked at him, waiting for orders. But Jesus remained silent, continuing to ponder, and nobody dared to interrupt his thoughts.

Judas returned from the village, carrying a bag of groceries. Jesus looked at Judas: young, strong Judas was cheerful and carefree. Jesus turned away from him, not wanting inadvertently to let Judas see that he was pondering and extremely conflicted.

Jesus felt extremely sorry for the young man. Would he be able be stay among the apostles after completing his task? Unfortunately, none of them would believe that Judas was executing the will of the Heavenly Father. After all, they still did not understand what their purpose was on the Earth, so how could they believe in the truth of Judas' words? It was a terribly unenviable task that was waiting for Judas. Jesus felt very badly, but there was no other way. His Father's plans must be implemented!

"Teacher, the sun is high. Is it time to continue our journey?" James, the brother of John Zebedee asked.

"Gather. We continue our journey."

The journey to the first rest was long. Immersed in his thoughts, Jesus was not feeling tired. The whole group was tired, but no one complained. If the teacher kept going, the group followed. Following the Teacher was always voluntarily; nobody was forced to walk in the sun on the barely visible road. Judas, as usual, walked behind the group. His burden was heavy, his sandals were worn, and his back ached, but Judas was happy that he had the honor of listening to the Teacher, to learn from him and to follow him. It was a fair compensation for the severity of the burden.

Jesus suddenly stopped and looked at the group. He did not see Judas, fenced off from Jesus by the crowd of followers. Jesus became alarmed and asked:

"Where is Judas Iscariot?"

"Teacher, as always he is behind," John said, and he shouted: "Hey, Judas, the teacher calls you."

The crowd parted, allowing Judas to walk ahead. Judas, bending under the weight of the burden, walked slowly toward Jesus. Jesus looked at the face of Judas; it was covered in sweat. .

"Let us relax," Jesus said. "We will rest here for an hour or two."

The disciples created a temporary camp. Someone brought firewood and began to prepare the broth. Everyone who was not involved in the preparations spread out their mats and lay down in the small bits of shade created by the olive trees that grew on the hillside.

John looked jealously at Judas. How to explain Jesus' attention to this Iscariot? Why did Jesus ask for him? Had Judas *earned* his attention? John knew that jealousy was one of the sins of man, but he could do nothing to overcome this adverse feeling. He wanted so much that Jesus would choose *him* to be his favorite disciple! Sometimes John thought that he had achieved this honor, but it cost Jesus to pay attention to someone as a feeling of insecurity in the love of Jesus become burning soul of John.

On this day, when Jesus asked about Judas, John glared at Judas as he caught up from behind. What did Jesus see in him? To John, Judas was an outsider; it was unknown how he had even become a member of their group. Judas meanwhile gladly stretched out on his mat, turning his hairy back to the sun and ignoring any disfavor on the part of his comrades. He was so tired that he was ready to go to sleep without even waiting for the women to prepare the chowder.

Judas' rest was stopped before it started. Jesus came to Judas and indicated that he wanted Judas to go with him. Judas understood the gesture of the Teacher and got to his feet. Jesus headed away from the fire to the top of the hill and Judas obediently followed. Fatigue almost drowned the joy that the teacher had invited him to walk with him. Judas rarely heard the busy Teacher mention his name, and the honor of a one-on-one conversation had never occurred before this day. John and Peter, the beloved disciples, sometimes talked with the teacher one-on-one, but Judas had never had the honor, and he never would have dared to ask the Teacher for this privilege. Anticipating the importance of the conversation, Judas obediently followed Jesus, feeling nervous as he walked.

Jesus sat down at the top of the hill, inviting Judas to sit beside him. Judas did not dare to sit down. He saw the other apostles at the foot of the hill watching him and he did not want to excite their envy.

"Sit down, friend Judas." Jesus said. "I need to talk to you."

"Teacher, down there the other pupils would find it a discourtesy towards you if I allowed myself to sit next to you."

"Do not be afraid of them. They are always jealous. It is a sin that needs to be cured, and it is an example that even good men are by nature sinful. A sinner has no place in paradise. How to help them? For the salvation of the souls of men, for the sake of making it possible for them to join the heavenly life, should not one suffer in this life? The heavenly Father commanded: 'Love thy neighbor!' I love the people who are close to me, and all the inhabitants of the earth. For the sake of the people, I am ready to suffer on this earth. What about you, Judas? Are you ready to offer the most sacred thing you have for the benefit of the people on earth?"

Judas was surprised. "You have me confused, my teacher. What sacred thing do I have? I really have nothing."

"Do not say this. Everyone has honor and a good name. It is the only sacred thing that every person has. For the sake of humanity, are you able and willing to lose your honor?" Jesus asked.

"For humanity? Do you mean for all the people on Earth? That purpose is huge and noble. For that I am ready to sacrifice my life!" Judas said fervently.

"Earthly life is a temporary phenomenon only," Jesus said thoughtfully. "Death comes sooner or later to all mortals. It is honor that is the eternal thing. I asked you not about life, but about your honor and your good name. The purpose is so important that for it someone must sacrifice *more* than their life – they must sacrifice their honor and their good name. Are you ready for such a sacrifice?"

Judas thought. He certainly did not consider himself so famous that someone would remember him even the day after his death. Perhaps one's mother and father would remember, but his were long gone— killed by the Romans. He did not understand what kind of memory Jesus was talking about.

"Teacher, I have no family; I have no wife or children. There is no one who would be interested in remembering me. No one will remember me on this earth after my death! My name will be forgotten the day after I am gone."

"You do not know this. I know that if you will do what is assigned to you, your name will remain forever in the memory of people. However, it will not be a good memory. Your name will become a household name in all languages, and it will only cause bad associations in humans. All because people will never know that you did it for *them*, for *their* benefit. The heavenly Father expects this terrible sacrifice from you. So are you ready for this?"

"Teacher, I swear in the name of your heavenly Father, that for the sake of humanity, I will make any sacrifice that He requires of me."

"I believe you. To start, I am asking you to keep today's conversation a secret. If you or I reveal this secret, our ability to solve the problem that we are about to tackle will be thwarted. Now let us descend; everyone is waiting us before serving the meal."

Judas walked down the hill thinking about the unknown task that the Heavenly Father wanted to assign to him. What was it that would cause him to lose his honor and remain in human memory as a terrible man? How could this be? He thought of King Herod, whose name was used to frighten children. Would he take the lives of thousands of innocent people as Herod had? A chill ran through the body of Judas. Would he kill people for the sake of their salvation? No, that could not happen, and it would be impossible anyway because he had no army. No, that was not the teacher meant. But what did he mean?

Three
The Reflections of Judas

JESUS AND HIS followers walked through a village that had a bad reputation. The pilgrims that journeyed to Jerusalem usually chose to bypass this particular village. In the morning, the women warned Jesus that in the village lived evil people willing to rob peaceful pilgrims. They feared neither God nor God's punishment for their crimes.

"I need to talk to these people." Jesus said. "Good must conquer evil."

"I beg you, please leave this village aside, as everyone does." Mary Magdalene said.

"I cannot. My goal is to correct evil. I have to instruct these people on the right path."

So they went directly through the village, as Jesus wished. The village was quiet and deserted. Even the dogs did not bark, hiding in holes. The silence and the solitude were chilling.

The procession walked slowly and peacefully. Ahead of the group was Jesus, followed by everyone else. Judas, bent under his burden, was as always at the back of the crowd, and by the time they had reached the last house, he had fallen a little behind the group. From the house in front of Judas came four strangers, armed with heavy sticks. They blocked the road in front of Judas.

"Give us your bag!" they demanded.

"You are asking the impossible, good people," Judas told them gently. "In this bag I carry our common money. It does not belong to me and I cannot give it to you."

"Money! That's what we want!" one of the strangers said and swung his club.

Judas, with one hand holding the bag, grabbed the stick with his other hand and pulled it out of the hands of the robber.

"I told you that these are not my things. Our common funds are in there so I cannot give them to you. Do you not understand me?"

The robbers surrounded Judas, and one of them took out a long knife and threatened Judas. This angered Judas. Continuing to hold the bag in one hand, he clubbed the arm of the robber so strongly that the robber lost his knife. The robber shouted in surprise and pain. Judah grabbed the baton from another robber, and swinging it, he stepped on the knife lost by the robber. Then he dropped the bag and picked up the knife in his left hand. By this time, Simon the Zealot stood next to Judas, waving his long dagger.

The whole group came to the cries of the apostles as the two disciples were ready to fight the four robbers. The robbers threw their batons away and tried to run away, but they could not, being surrounded by the crowd.

Jesus walked in. "Good people!" he said. "Do you need some money? Judas, give each of them a silver coin. We are not greedy and we do not for ourselves alone collect donations. Good people, you live on this earth and you must not violate the laws of God. It is time to quit your evil deeds and heed the word of God. For those who truly believe, there will always be a piece of daily bread. As is said: 'It will be a day, there will be food!' Pray for the salvation of your soul!"

Judas opened the sack, took out a cash drawer, and gave one silver coin to each of the robbers. The robbers, knowing that they were caught and deserved punishment, marveled at the generosity of Jesus. His appeal to them not as criminals but as lost souls, struck them to the depth of their soul. They were ashamed to take Judas' money.

"Take it, good people," Judas said. "The giver's hand will not become scanty. I am sorry, brother, that I hit your hand so strongly that it swelled up. Truly I hit not from malice, believe me."

Judas tied the bag and threw it on his back. The whole procession continued on, discussing the incident.

"Look at this Judas Iscariot," Thaddeus said to Thomas. "As soon as Jesus talked to him one-on-one, he became polite and even apologized to the robber. Where did this guy learn courtesy? None other than Jesus scolded him there, on top of the hill. His face was painfully unhappy when they came down from the hill."

"Of course he was scolded. Jesus does not like to scold in front of people so he led him to the top of the hill," Said Thomas. "You're right, Judas was gloomy and thoughtful, confused by the words of the Master."

"He looked like a beaten dog," Said Thaddeus.

Marching behind them, Mary Magdalene said, "No, I think he just looked respectful. Jesus did not scold him. Jesus himself was frowning thoughtfully."

"Yes, he was scolded," Thomas said confidently. "Do you women get pleasure if you are forced to curse someone? Naturally, the teacher was not glad."

It was sunset when the group came to the place that Jesus had indicated as their overnight stop. Everyone in the group set up their mats and they were ready for evening prayer, waiting for the signal from Jesus. Jesus, lost in his thoughts, was not in a hurry to give a sign.

Mary Magdalene prepared to light the evening candles. She gently touched the hands of Jesus, recalling the beginning of the Sabbath. Jesus looked up from his thoughts, and said: "Blessed is a new day."

This was the expected signal. Women started to pray, lighting the candles. The Saturday meal began. This Saturday it was leaner than usual. Judas ate quickly and only waited for the signal to end of the meal. The morning revelation of Jesus excited him. He could not imagine the mission, which Jesus was going to entrust him. The eternal damnation of descendants, with which Jesus frightened him, did not bother his soul. He was young and he had no family, no children. Why should he care what strangers would think about him after his death? He worried much more about what the Heavenly Father of Jesus and the angels in heaven would think about him. If he could complete the task successfully, then the angels in heaven would treat him with respect, knowing that he was on a mission trusted to him by God's son. It was worth it to sacrifice his reputation on Earth in exchange for obtaining a good reputation in Heaven. He did not know the essence of the mission that Jesus would entrust to him, and he was worried about his ability to execute it. Did he have enough strength, intelligence, dexterity?

Jesus, too, was immersed in thought. He now wondered how to make himself a deadly dangerous man in the eyes of the High Priests. The temple priests had to be imbued with such fear that it would be impossible for them to leave Jesus alive. There were plenty of stray preachers in Judea. The High Priests, though they did not love these preachers, really didn't worry much whether there was one more or less. It would be necessary to do something that really seemed threatening to them. How could he make the High Priests see him as a mortal enemy, while at the same time not violate any laws nor ethics of the earth.

Jesus knew well that in people's minds, he must remain a model of morality, a symbol of truth and hope. But at the same time he had to convince the priests that he was dangerous for them. Jesus' deeds should always be directed to fight against evil. In the eyes of ordinary people, those who sent Jesus to death should personify as an evil. It should be obvious even to the most ignorant people, from those whom the apostles would attract in the bosom of the Faith. People need to believe that the Lord allowed the suffering of his innocent Son for the sake of the human race, to save their souls from eternal suffering in Hell.

Jesus prayed to his Father, asking the Father to show him the right way to achieve this goal. Jesus decided that miracles unclear to mortals would excite the anger of the Pharisees and the High Priest. Good miracles would not dishonor his name and they would give confidence to those who witnessed these miracles. He should continue to do miracles.

However, would this be enough to incite the hatred of the Pharisees? He knew that the temple priests would not like miracles, but this would not be enough to make the High Priest hate him. Many stray tricksters with various tricks, walked along the roads. All sorts of people walked the roads. Always the priests were able to convince the crowd that miracles were actually just tricks, sleight of hand and illusions, Miracles, no matter how extraordinary they might be, were only partly dangerous to the priests. Then it dawned on Jesus. He should declare himself the *King* of the Jews, who came to earth not to *rule* people, but to open the True Faith to the people, whom the priests of Jerusalem were leading in the wrong direction.

This claim would be dangerous for the High Priest. He, Jesus, as a descendant of King David, had more right to the position of the spiritual Head of the nation than all the Levites together. Joseph, the earthly father of Jesus, was a descendant of King David. From Abraham, the founder of the Jewish tribes, to King David there were descendants of exactly fourteen generations; and from King David to the exile of the Jews to Babylon fourteen generations exactly, and from the deportation of the Jews to the time of Jesus, fourteen generations. Every fourteen generations, as history shows, there happens something that radically changes the life of all the people of Judah. Jesus knew that now the moment had come when God sent to mankind his Son, whose task was to bring all humanity to the true faith.

The teachings that attributed the right to salvation only to the chosen people were erroneous. The Creator, our Lord and Master, points the way to salvation; not the priests of the Jerusalem Temple. The temple in Jerusalem, serving only the people of Judah, was not capable of coping with the task of familiarizing all the people on earth with the true faith. The idea that salvation can come to all people on earth contradicted the teachings of the priests in the Temple.

According to the teachings of Jesus, the Temple priests were not needed for salvation. Salvation would come to those who had faith in the one Creator and who lived a righteous life. Preachers anywhere on earth could direct people to the knowledge of the True faith; they did not have to be in the Jerusalem Temple. What's more, the Jerusalem Temple and its priests, who did not live a righteous life, could not be an example of knowledge of the truth.

As soon as the priests found out that Jesus was teaching people that the Temple priests only *prevented* people from knowing the truth about faith, they would want to get rid of the Prophet by passing him over to the mercy of the Romans.

Jesus was satisfied with his insight. He had no doubt that his Heavenly Father had sent him this knowledge. Jesus was going to fulfill his destiny. It was very frightening for him to expose his body to be afflicted, but it was clearly the only way to fulfill his earthly mission, according to the wishes of his Heavenly Father.

The next morning Jesus told Mary Magdalene about his royal origins, telling her that he intended to apply for recognition of his rights by all the people of the Roman province of Judea. He knew that no one better than a woman could cope with the disclosure of a secret, if you wanted many more people to know the secret. And indeed, after an hour all twelve apostles learned the secret. They openly discussed the news, and many of the crowd following them heard their conversations. Those who had been sent from Jerusalem to follow the new prophet also heard the news.

The pharisaical spies felt that the news was important enough to be conveyed as an urgent message to the ears of Anna, the High Priest and the head of the Sanhedrin. One of the spies went to Jerusalem, and Jesus was pleased to see it, and he saw everything that happened. John, one of Jesus' apostles, also noticed that one of the members of the crowd rushed to break away from the group. He realized that it was an unfriendly act toward their beloved teacher, and he decided to catch the spy.

Jesus stopped John: "Dear friend John. One sheep will not run away from of herd. Let the person go in peace. He will be back, believe me."

"He is a spy from the Pharisees. He goes to reveal our secrets to his friends the Pharisees," John replied.

"Do not worry about it. We have no secrets that we would like to hide from humans. We walk on this earth not to hide secrets, but to educate people. The more people know the truth, the better we will serve the Lord."

"I do not like the person who left us." John said.

"We are going to reveal the truth to all people—to those we like, and those we dislike."

John did not go to catch the spy; he stayed among the followers of Jesus.

Mary came to Jesus and said: "We are approaching my home village. Usually we do not spend the night in the village. Would you make an exception this time? Do you not wish to stay in the house of my sister Martha?"

"How can I refuse you and your lovely relatives?" Jesus replied. "This time we will stay within the village."

They stayed within Mary's native village. Judas was glad that this time he did not have to sleep on the stones of the desert, but rather under the roof of the hospitable villagers.

The people of the village came to pay their respects to the renowned and esteemed teacher. Thanks to the relatives of Mary, the whole village knew about the works of Jesus and anxiously awaited a miracle. But Jesus was very tired from the road and he was hungry. He put his hand in the air for his blessing and frankly confessed his fatigue and hunger. One of the richest inhabitants, one Jonah the tax-gatherer, invited Jesus into his house to have dinner with him and his loved ones, saying: "In my house you will find hospitality and a hearty meal worthy of you."

Jesus agreed and allowed himself to be led into the house of Jonah. In those days, people ate dinner lying down. Jonah offered Jesus a couch in the place of honor next to him, and several distinguished guests settled down for the meal with Jesus. Judas and the other apostles were not invited to this dinner. They had dinner at the home of Lazarus, the brother of Martha. And they were treated to the simple dishes of peasants—lentil soup and fresh bread.

At dinner, John told his friends the apostles: "Strangely, our teacher always says that honor must be given to poor people, and today he agreed to go for dinner at the house of this fat tax-gatherer."

Peter supported John. "You're right. This act is contrary to what the Master teaches us."

"Do you not trust the teacher?" Judas protested. "Jesus always has a purpose to anything that he does. Jesus never decides because of selfish reasons. We must believe the teacher, always and everywhere, because he said, one is saved who believes!"

"The teacher is an earthly man," said Andrew. "It is necessary to believe in the Creator! Earthly people tend to be wrong; they can wish ill and commit other sins. Man is sinful; only the Heavenly Father is sinless."

"You do not understand!" Judas was outraged. "Jesus is not an earthly man—he is the Son of the Heavenly Father. We always have to believe and unconditionally fulfill all that he asks for, even if it brings unbearable pain."

The apostles reacted with disbelief to the words of Judas. It was commendable that this Judas blindly trusted the teacher, but as Andrew explained: "One should remember the saying, 'Trust in God, but remember that He helps those who help themselves.' In addition, if Jesus would want to make a joke about any of us, should we help him to make fun of us? No, everyone should first think, and then do what is asked only if he will not be laughed at."

Judas pondered the job that Jesus was going to charge him with. What was the job that could bring him eternal damnation on earth? After thinking a bit, Judas concluded that since life on earth is not eternal, so the curse on earth could not be eternal. Someday the truth would be revealed, and his name would no longer be a shameful symbol. This thought reassured him.

Meanwhile, by the end of dinner at the home of Jonah arrived a woman who asked the house members to allow her to see Jesus. Jonah's wife did not want to allow a woman to see the prophet, considering her as a sinner unworthy of beholding a saint. Her refusal caused an uproar, which came to the ears of Jesus, and Jesus asked that the woman be brought to him. The woman came in and knelt at the feet of Jesus.

"Rabbi!" the woman said, "I am so grateful to you that I cannot find the words to adequately express my gratitude. I would wash your feet with my tears of gratitude!"

Everyone present looked in disbelief at the woman. However, she started to cry and her eyes shed tears on Jesus' feet. Then she began to wipe the tears with her marvelous long hair. Then she took a jug of oil of nard and smeared the tired legs of Jesus with the oil. It was the highest form of love and gratitude and so unusual that all those present rose from their beds. Jesus did not need to explain why there was such gratitude; he knew the reason.

Jonah indignantly said to himself: "No, he is not a prophet. The Prophet would immediately determine that this woman is sinful, unworthy of communion with the saints." Jonah was surprised and outraged by the behavior of the woman. In his house, he saw only himself as worthy of this honor. Jesus, though, was the guest of honor, but he was a beggar, a wandering preacher. Was it possible to compare this prophet with Jonah, the richest resident of the village?

Jesus read the thoughts of Jonah and he said, smiling: "Wealth is not a sign of dignity, dear Jonah. Only those who put faith above wealth are worthy of this honor. Abandon wealth and devote yourself to serving the cause of faith, and you will deserve eternal bliss. This woman has washed my feet with tears, and what have you done? Have you filled me even with plain water? Do you smear my head with oil? In addition, she has greased my feet with expensive oil. She showed kindness, and because of this, all her sins are forgiven her."

Jesus turned to the woman and said to her: "You showed everyone that you believe in me. Because of your faith, all your sins are forgiven. Go in peace."

The guests were surprised at his forgiveness of sins. Was he a saint or a simple preacher? By what right did he forgive sins? With fear and respect, they looked at Jesus. Was he really a saint?

That same evening, Mary Magdalene secretly told her sister and brother the origins of Jesus from King David. Martha was not surprised. She asked Mary: "Do you know the origin of his mother, Mary?"

"No, I do not know."

"So you should know that she comes from the distant branches of the Hasmoneans. The truly royal blood is flowing in your Teacher. You should be happy that such a man has drawn attention to you, made you close to him and loved you."

"I love him to the depths of my soul and my whole life is dedicated to this man. But my heart feels that the Pharisees will give him no rest. That is the source of my worries."

Four
The High Priest Kiafa

THE HIGH PRIEST Anna sat on a high chair at his home in the upper town. He thought about the fate of his people, who were experiencing a very difficult time. The Roman invaders acted as if the people of the country were their property. He, the leader of the Sanhedrin, had to stoop before this ignorant pagan Pontius Pilate. Pontius Pilate was unclear regarding many of the strict rules of Judaism. What a pain it was to try and convince him to take off from their banners the image of the Emperor of Rome. Anna took a long time to explain to the procurator that Judaism does not allow any images at all, and that this was not directed against the Emperor or Rome. Pontius Pilate did not understand the concept of a single God. He believed that there were many gods and that the Emperor was one of them! Anna recalled how Pontius Pilate had laughed loudly at the claim that there was just one God for all. Under these conditions, it was not possible to convince him that God, common to all peoples of the world, chose the Jewish people.

"Do not make me laugh, stupid Jew." Pontius Pilate had said upon hearing Anna's explanation. "Your tribal God, Yahweh, is a very weak God if he has allowed your people to become vassals of mighty Rome. No, do not compare the strength of our Gods with yours. Your God is a pitiful beggar on the divine Olympus.

Thank God, we managed to persuade Pilate to remove the image of the Emperor, Anna said to himself. Later, when Pontius Pilate in Jerusalem had decided to build a water supply system, it was not so easy to calm down the people who objected to this innovation. The people were impoverished and with great difficulty making ends meet during the years of Roman rule. The people were seething with discontent with the Roman government, and the descendants of Herod the Great could not keep control of the state. The united country of Judah no longer existed. Under these conditions, many of the Jews gladly listened to sermons of any self-appointed preachers, as they excited people and warmed the crowd to disobey the authorities. Then the Zealots appeared in the country, hiding their daggers under their clothing and at every opportunity committing the murder of Roman soldiers.

There was a soft knock, and Isaac, one of the guards of the Sanhedrin, came into the room. He politely stood in front of Anna, not daring to break the train of thought of the head of the Sanhedrin.

"What happened?" Anna asked.

"One of our people, who is keeping an eye on the activities of Jesus the preacher, came with a message worthy of your ears."

"Let him come," Anna allowed.

In a room lit by a single candle came a spy, who had recently left a group of people wandering with Jesus. He barely saw Anna and bowed before the great man.

"At the camp of this beggar Jesus of Nazareth, the rumor was told that Jesus imagined himself as king of Judea. He told his disciples that he is a descendant of King David and that he has come to demand the throne of his great ancestor. We decided to communicate this news to your ears."

"What else can you add?"

"That's all."

"Go back and continue to follow him."

Anna called his adviser Elijah. Elijah was so named in honor of the great prophet. He was a very knowledgeable person and a close relative of Anna.

"Did you hear that?" Anna asked, knowing well that Elijah was in the next room all the time and could hear everything that was said in the chambers of Anna.

"Yes, I heard," Elijah said. "And do you know what is the best part?"

"What?"

"This Jesus, son of Joseph the carpenter of Nazareth, really comes from one of the tribes of David. I checked it a long time ago, when he appeared at the River Jordan with a request that John the Baptist cleanse him in the waters of the Jordan. Then this John showed such great honor to this beggar that I felt it necessary to learn all about him. And the mother of this Jesus is of royal blood too, according to my sources. She is a distant relative to the house of the Hasmoneans, the Levites."

"Do you think he can bring trouble to our people?" Anna asked.

"Our people are in such dire straits, so excited that any preacher can easily throw a spark in dry hay. So far as I know, he preaches only absolute faith in God. The information that he calls for a struggle with the authorities did not reach us."

"Do not tell me!" Anna interrupted. "I had a report that among his disciples is one by the name of Simon the Zealot. While he does not call for an uprising, everything is possible. We must be on our guard."

"Yes, his teaching could be dangerous. He preaches that only the rich in spirit and the poor materially are loved by God. So look, he may call for the rejection of wealth by force. I am concerned about the fact that he does not believe that God chooses only Jews. He preaches that all those who believe in one God and observe the commandments of Moses are chosen by God for eternal bliss."

"He's a dangerous man. This way he could declare that the priests of the Temple are not important and that the priests are not mandatory for bringing sacrifices for purification before God."

"He's a menace to society," Elijah confirmed. "We need to get rid of him."

"You think so?" Anna raised his eyebrows.

"We have enough worries without him," Elijah said. "The people listen to Jesus and this is dangerous. The sooner we get rid of him, the better. We as individuals are responsible to our people; we cannot allow adversity to come upon our people, and that could happen if we do not stop this beggar descendant of King David. Our country is weak now. We cannot afford a war with Rome. Judea would not withstand the second Babylon."

"I'll think about it," Anna said.

Anna thought. He needed to consult with Kiafa. Kiafa was the acting High Priest and Anna did not want to make decisions without the approval of the head of the Temple. Kiafa was the son-in-law of Anna. He always listened to the words of Anna, who was highly experienced, but this time the case seemed very dangerous to Anna, with unknown consequences. Such decisions had to be made in concert with the acting High Priest himself.

At the house of Kiafa, Anna found a visiting guest, Tetrarch Herod Antipas. The host and guest were lying on luxury couches when the servants announced the arrival of Anna.

Kiafa said: "Dear Anna, Herod came to see us. He came to discuss his concerns about rumors that instead of John the Baptist, who preached at the Jordan River some stupid propaganda, there is a new popular preacher named Jesus, who took the cleansing waters of the Jordan, and this preacher stirs up the people by preaching about salvation. Herod is struggling to settle conflicts with this stubborn procurator of Judea, Pontius Pilate, and he does not want a new preacher stirring up the people against him and the great Roma."

"I have come to you to discuss the same issue," Anna said. "In addition to his outrageous sermons, Jesus now declares himself a descendant of King David, which to our knowledge is true. He wants to claim the ancestral rights to Judea, Samaria, and all the land that once belonged to the kingdom of David and his son Solomon."

"The descendants of David lost their rights to the throne after the conquest of Jerusalem by Babylon!" Herod said.

"You're right, Herod. But now, since you lost your rights under the influence of Rome, the throne of Judah is free to the heirs of the royal families," Anna said, taking his place on the couch. "The only trouble is that this throne trampled Rome and Rome is not going to give it to anyone."

"I'm gonna kill this Jesus as I killed John!" Herod Antipas said.

"Do not get excited, Herod," Kiafa said. "This would not return to you the throne of Herod the Great. You should not fight with the preacher, who has influence among the common people. Your task is to convince people that you are on the side of the ordinary people of the kingdom that was taken away from you. While Judah is a Roman province, your strength is in popular support. Only with the support of the people can you hope to get from Rome the full ownership of Judea. You should make Pontius Pilate guilty of turbulence in Judea in the eyes of the Emperor. Rome should know that because of Pilate's unreasonable actions, Judea has the perturbation. Do you understand me?"

"You are wise, Kiafa. No wonder you were elected High Priest!" Herod said.

"I agree that it is necessary to see the Romans as the villains in the eyes of our people," Anna said.

"I am afraid that the preaching of Jesus will cause the indignation of the people, and then spill a lot of blood. The whole question is how to get rid of this harmful preacher before he becomes powerful and dangerous, and in a way that will not cause the suffering of a lot of innocent people. Whom will your serve, Kiafa, if the Roman thugs drown Judea in blood? We need a trick to prevent people from rising to a struggle with Rome. Believe me; the Jews have no strength to fight with the mighty Rome. Let people stay outraged, but not enough to shed more blood."

"I agree," said Kiafa. "How to implement it?"

"That's what I came for. First, the Romans should eliminate Jesus. Second, they should not kill him as a preacher, a holy man, but as a simple criminal, a man who doesn't obey the laws of Rome. The penalty should happen without noise and without widely alerting the people. The Romans should execute him as the Romans usually do. The Romans execute many criminals each year. No one except for a narrow circle of relatives and close friends should be allowed to the place of execution. The less people know about the capture and execution of Jesus, the less the perturbation will be. This is necessary for the safety of the people."

"What do you need for this?" Herod Antipas asked eagerly.

"We should not arrest Jesus in the daytime when he is surrounded by people. The arrest should be at night when just a few people will know about the arrest.

"You're right, dear Anna," Kiafa said. "I will work with Pontius Pilate and ask him to make sure that he doesn't make a mess of this and to not announce publicly the impending execution. It would be better if nobody knows about the execution. But Jesus has disciples, and they will try to continue his work. What do you advise to do with them?"

"I think that they will be frightened by the death of Jesus," replied Anna. It will take time before they try to continue his sermons. Jesus is said to be a very talented orator. Although he is the son of a carpenter and a simple man who did not study in the Academy, he easily quotes the Torah and my people cannot argue with him, even where they are convinced of the correctness. He is very dangerous. But His disciples are not enlightened people and are often inarticulate. They will not be able to replace him. The educated Jews will not follow them. We are not barbarians; we should not bring them to death just because they are followers of a gifted preacher. Let them live as they can."

"And if they continue his preaching?" Kiafa asked.

"At first, they will have listeners. But as time passes, people will get tired of listening to them," Anna said. "Among them there is no talent such as Jesus. They are not dangerous to our people."

"Well, we will follow your advice," Kiafa said. "But we will need eyes in front and behind them. Who knows, maybe they will attract someone very talented to their side? This cannot be allowed."

"Why do you indulge them!" Herod exclaimed. "They should all be destroyed! We do not need any preachers, talented or ignorant. They are all parasites and troublemakers!"

"You're impatient, sir," Kiafa replied calmly. "With your behavior you can cause more problems than these modest preachers. Who asked you to demonstratively present the head of John to Salome your stepdaughter? You know that killing is a sin. If you take on your soul the sin of killing unwanted subjects, then do it without noise. You should have killed him quietly, not stirred up protests. You forget that your goal is not to kill the Jews, but to unite them around you."

"You advise me dangerously,' retorted Herod. When in Rome, I learned that if I unite people around me, very soon they will find a place for me somewhere in Britain in exile, away from the people who love me. Popular support also needs to have boundaries so as not to incur the wrath of Rome."

"Herod is right," Anna said. "All needs to be measured. A little bit of people love and a little bit of hatred. We must maneuver in this life."

"You tell me when you get rid of Jesus," Herod said impatiently. "I do not want some poor descendant of a long-forgotten dynasty claiming my throne. Hurry! I do not want to wait long. I want his head."

"Be patient," Kiafa said. "In such a case we must not unduly hurry. Trouble can descend on our unfortunate people. Be patient."

"Listen to me, Herod," Anna said. "You should stay away from this business. Leave it to us. We do not want any civil unrest. We will make sure that even the inhabitants of Jerusalem learn the fate of the preacher after the execution. Moreover, when they find out, they should accuse the Roman governor, not us. Got that?"

"Well, you are both pettifoggers. You want to achieve all this with cunning. And Rome to please and appease the people," said Herod. "Okay, let it be your way. I'm not going to do anything, but I cannot endure forever this pretender to my throne."

"What throne? You have no throne!" Kiafa was outraged. "Did you forget that you're a vassal of Rome? It may hurt you, but you should understand that the issue is not *you*. If the people rise up, it will not be about returning you to the throne. It will be rebellion against Rome, the mighty Rome drowned in the blood not only of our people, but also of your whole dynasty. Do you want to march in chains in Rome at the next triumphant procession? Do you understand what we, along with my father-in-law fear?"

"You, Kiafa, draw a very bleak picture," Herod said soothingly. "I authorize you to resolve the current situation."

"You authorize?" Kiafa said angrily. "No, you are not in charge. It is a responsibility that I put on myself when I was elected High Priest, to save our people from harm, which may bring frivolous rebellion against Rome. Go with God, Sir, and give us the freedom to make decisions that will save our people, our Temple, and our way of life."

Herod rose from his couch, and clearly unhappy with Kiafa's rebuke, left the High Priest's house. He was angry with Kiafa. "Just think how important this Kiafa considers himself to be! If not for Rome, he would have kissed my feet." Herod did not care about the suffering of the Jewish people. He was hurt that damn Rome had deprived him of the glory and power that belonged to him by his inheritance.

Five

The Affairs of Jesus

THROUGHOUT JUDEA, THE rumor circulated that although Herod had beheaded John the Baptist, the saint had been reborn in the person of Jesus of Nazareth, who had the power to heal and cast out demons. The rumor wandered around the country and even reached the ears of Jesus and his apostles. The apostles were surprised listening to the rumors. Some people saw in Jesus John the Baptist, and some the prophet Elijah. The disciples discussed this among themselves: "Jesus sends us to heal people, and to tell them the truth about the Creator, and to inspire people to obey the rules of morality and conscience. And we do what we have never been able to do before, and everything that he sends us to do, we do well. So who is Jesus that he has the power to make of us, simple fishermen, healers that are able to heal people successfully? Where is this power in him? Look at him—he is not a mighty athlete and he does not look like a sage, but he teaches and his words go into one's soul so deeply that after his preaching there remains no doubt about the truth of his teachings."

Judas was surprised by this discussion. "Do you not understand that he is the Son of God? Truly, I say that his power is not from his human mother, but from his Heavenly Father."

Jesus did not hear them talk about this because they conducted the talk only when he was not with them, but he knew that his disciples were discussing him. Of course, all students discuss their teacher behind their back. But at this point Jesus himself decided to talk with the disciples about himself, and about the fate that awaited him. He gathered up all the apostles, seated them in front of him, and asked:

"My trusted disciples, tell me what people say about me."

"They say you're a resurgent John who baptized people in the waters of the Jordan," Peter said.

"Others say that you are the prophet Elijah returned to earth to educate people and guide them to the right path," said Andrew.

"There are those who think you're one of the great prophets of the past, come down to earth from heaven," said John.

"What do you, my faithful disciples, think about me?" Jesus asked.

All the disciples were modestly silent. Even Judas, looking at the teacher with adoring eyes, did not dare say anything.

In the ensuing awkward silence, Jesus calmly looked at the apostles waiting for an answer. "So what do *you* think?" Jesus repeated, with emphasis on the word *you*.

Peter stood up, bowed to the teacher, and said: "We are taking you for the Christ of God."

"Dear friends. I ask that you do not tell anybody about this. Agreed? I have to face in front of me a very hard time. The Elders and Pharisees will reject me. It will not be easy to win the minds of humanity to my teaching. A thousand years will come, but not all people on earth will accept me. However, most will believe in me. Until then, I will have to die after first suffering. On the third day after my death, I will rise again.

But the way before *you* will also be difficult, my friends. Anyone who chooses to go through this difficult life should know that you will have to endure suffering. Whoever is afraid of this and wants to keep his body will lose his soul. Who is not afraid to go my way, through death and suffering, will have an eternal soul. In this life, everyone has to carry his burden, no matter how difficult it may be."

The apostles listened to their teacher and did not understand the deep meaning of his words. Judas was the only one who knew that in the future his name would be cursed on the earth if he fulfilled the unknown task that Jesus was going to require of him. And therein lay the burden that he would bear. Yes, he was ready for it. Jesus Christ was God, and Judas was ready for any shame and any curse when Jesus beckoned.

"Some of you may be ashamed of me and of my words. You should know that anyone who is ashamed of the Son of man, I will be ashamed of when it comes to the time of glory for my Father and me. And there are some of you who would know the kingdom of God while still alive!" Jesus added, looking directly at the wide eyes of Judas.

After these words, Jesus wanted climb to the nearby hill and pray. He took with him Peter, John, and James, and together with them slowly ascended the hill. There he devoted himself to prayer. The apostles were surprised to notice how the face of Jesus changed while he was praying, and his clothes suddenly brightened and became shiny, reflecting in their brilliance the proximity of the man to whom the prayer was addressed. Truly, Jesus was the Messiah, the anointed by God. And Jesus asked God, his Father, to hasten the day when he would reunite with his Father, promising to bravely endure the torments that were inevitable and necessary for reunification with the Father.

It was not clear to the apostles why, in order to reunite with the Heavenly Father, Jesus must suffer. Would a loving father wish torment upon his son? Jesus was great, but incomprehensible to ordinary people. However, there must be some hidden meaning in these torments, if the suffering was so important to the Heavenly Father. They wanted to ask Jesus but they did not dare.

On the way down the hill, the apostles worried about their teacher. And they pondered the words of Jesus: that those who save their soul actually lose, and those who do not spare their life will be saved. What did that mean?

"Explain, teacher, please the meaning of your phrase about salvation?" John dared to ask.

"When I talked about salvation, I did not mean the salvation of the body. Those who are afraid and rush to save their body will destroy their immortal soul. Those who would not spare for the truth their body will find eternal salvation. Do you understand?"

"Now I understand."

At the foot of the hill, the rest of the apostles were waiting for them. They were all waiting for the continuation of the lecture, but Jesus wanted to be alone. He was thoughtful and sad. Despite the pain he would suffer, he wanted to quickly reunite with his father. Jesus withdrew, leaving the apostles in deep thought.

Simon the Zealot was completely unclear as to how the Messiah returned to earth but did not talk about the liberation of Israel from the foreign yoke. In his mind, this was the purpose of Christ, the Messiah, the anointed of God. He should follow the example of Moses, who freed the people from slavery in Egypt. He should bring to Rome such executions so that Rome, with all its might, would leave the Jews alone. Yet Jesus talked about suffering and his own death. It was very strange. Simon shared his thoughts with his comrades.

"I share your opinion, dear Simon," Philip said. "Now, when the people of Israel suffer badly under the Roman invaders, the task of the Messiah should be the liberation of God's chosen people, the Jews."

"You both do not understand," Peter explained. "This time the Messiah came to this earth not for just one nation of Israel. He came for the salvation of all mankind. Mankind is steeped in sin and never will deserve the support of God if they are not freed from their sins. *All* sins. Why do you think that your friends the Zealots are better than the Romans? They violate the main Commandment: 'Thou shalt not kill!' No, not just our people need to be saved, but all of Mankind. That is the mission of Jesus."

"Verily so!" Judas confirmed. He had listened to Peter with profound attention.

"How would Jesus achieve this?" John asked.

"First, we need to convince all the people that God is one, and the belief in many different gods, who themselves are ready to sin, is disrespectful to the Creator," Peter said proudly. "This sermon the Jews do not need; they already believe in one God. However, Jesus came not just for the Jews; he came for all people on the Earth. We need to preach not only to Jews but also to the Gentiles."

"I disagree with you," Andrew said. "We, the Jews, are the chosen people. The first step is to absolve the Jews of their sins. And to you, Simon, I say that sinless people are not afraid of Rome. God will protect the sinless. My opinion is that we should not go to preach to the Gentiles until we cleanse from sin the Chosen people."

"What are you arguing, my friends?" John asked. "I think the teachings of our teacher Jesus are important for our people and the same for all the peoples on earth."

"You do not understand," Simon the Zealot insisted, "Jesus is going to suffer in order to cause all the people to fight against Rome. People will become indignant about the mockery of our prophet and everyone will rise to fight, both old and young! I think this is the earthly goal of Jesus."

Judas looked at Simon with contempt. This Zealot understands nothing, he said to himself. We are not talking about an uprising; Jesus did not seek to incite the people to fight. Any struggle would violate the principle of "do not kill." Judas remembered how Jesus once, to the provocation of the Pharisees, said, "Pay Caesar what is due to Caesar, and pay God what is due to God." Jesus recognizes the right of the King to his lot, so the right of Rome to conquer provinces. No, Jesus does not call for a fight with Rome; he encourages people to believe in one God, to believe in the true faith in compliance with all of the divine laws. And he does not fight with the pagans but with paganism; and not with the Pharisees, but with hypocrisy. His goal is to lead all people on earth to the true faith in one God.

The apostle Andrew noticed that Judas was anxiously absorbed in his thoughts and he decided to have some fun with Judas. In circumstances where the severity of the way and the learning was close to unbearable, a friendly joke would soothe the soul. Usually Judas was the subject of jokes, often when he was worried that the community would not have enough money to feed the apostles and those poor people who followed them. Judas usually took the jokes very seriously and reacted with anger. This amused the rest of the apostles, who were not averse to laughing at angry Judas when the joke was on him.

"Hey Judas," Andrew asked. "What are you thinking this time? Friends, he counts in his mind how much money is left in his box."

"Leave it be!" Judas said. "I have no time for money in the public treasury. Do not worry about money; somehow we will survive."

The joke had failed this time. Judas had not succumbed to provocation. A pity. Andrew so wanted to unburden himself by laughing! All the apostles were sad about Jesus' last lecture.

In the morning, Jesus joined the apostles and told them to continue their trip. He hastened to ascend to Jerusalem the week before the onset of the Passover holiday. All worshipers, by the laws of Moses, honor this holiday as the most important after Yom Kippur; and all believers in the holiday of Passover know the importance of making a sacrifice to God. By tradition, in Jerusalem only the Temple priests could perform the ritual of sacrifice on behalf of the worshipers. The blood of the Sacrificial Lamb spilled on the altar would clear the worshipers of sin.

For this holiday, huge crowds flocked to the temple. On those days, Jesus needed to go to the Temple to make known the appearance of the Messiah to more people. Jesus needed to announce to people that the sacrifices made by the sinful priests of the temple were not enough for the people to cleanse their soul before God. More important was the sacred water of the Jordan River; baptism by water was an important first step to get closer to God. Jesus knew that this preaching would be like a knife in the heart for the temple priests. It would strengthen their desire to bring Jesus to the Romans.

Jesus and his disciples came to the next village on their way, and a large group of village residents approached them. They drove before them a woman with cascading hair and tears on her face. Seeing Jesus and his companions, the group stopped. One of the group recognized Jesus, and supposing he was a prophet, said: "This woman was caught in adultery. We want to beat her with stones, as spelled out in the Law of Moses. What do you say, holy man?"

Jesus looked at the woman doomed to be stoned and silently began to draw with his stick on the ground. One of the Pharisees repeated impatiently:

"Say, Jesus from Nazareth in Galilee, should we beat the sinner caught in adultery?"

Jesus did not like the tone of the man who sought to trap Jesus in offense of the law. Jesus looked at the crowd of people and said confidently: "Let the man among you who is without sin cast the first stone." Then Jesus continued to draw signs in the earth.

The crowd of villagers, hearing his words, froze in disbelief. Everyone in his mind recalled his big and small sins. And there was no one who could not remember at least a minor sin. Ashamed, the people, one by one, turned and went back to the village, starting with the oldest and most respected and ending with the young and hot-headed. Only the woman stayed in front of Jesus and his companions, and she bowed her head before the holy man.

"Woman, where are your accusers?" Jesus asked.

"They are gone."

"Yes, they are all gone and not condemning you. I do not blame you. Go with God and sin no more."

Turning to the disciples, Jesus said: "Only those who are sinless can judge and accuse a man of committing sin. A quick trial committed under the influence of an angry crowd is one of the biggest sins of man. It is so easy to condemn the innocent. The Heavenly Father will never forgive the condemnation of the innocent by a judge blinded by emotion. The judge must be cold, just and fair."

The apostles, and others who heard him, believed in the truth of the words of Jesus and in his holiness. Jesus added: "With me you will know the truth and it will lead you to freedom."

This surprised the disciples and all who heard it. "Are we slaves?" they asked. "We are free descendants of Abraham and Jacob!"

"I know that you are Abraham's seed and that you do not reside in slavery," said Jesus. "You did not understand me. Who does not know the truth is a slave of darkness. There are among those following me the people who love me and want to learn about the truth and those who want to kill me."

The spies of Anna wondered how it happened that Jesus had learned about them. Their hearts fluttered from the danger of being unmasked when they were surrounded by the disciples of Jesus.

"And I say to those who do not believe in my teaching and in me, that I tell you the truth. I am the son of the Heavenly Father, and I came from God to you. I come not just by my own will, but by the will of He who sent me. I say to you: whoever observes my word shall never see death."

The Pharisees that were walking with him did not believe him. They considered as blasphemy the claim that Jesus was the Son of God. Yes, this man could do simple wonders, and maybe God transmitted some force to him; however, he was a human, not God's flesh and blood.

Even the apostles understood the words of Jesus not literally, but as a metaphor confirming the correctness of his teaching. They believed in Jesus, but in reality they were doubtful of his divine origin. Only Judas believed that Jesus was the Son of God.

Because of this, Jesus had entrusted to Judas the role that doubters could not perform. Others would argue: "What will happen? Is it right to do this? What will the other apostles think about me?"

No, they could not fulfill this task. They would be afraid, and they would be loath to lose their reputation among their comrades. In this case, it was necessary to have someone who would execute the task without hesitation, exactly as agreed.

Jesus said to himself: "The Heavenly Father sent Judas to me; he knows how to send the right people for whatever purpose, and Judas is strong and faithful. And Peter, who is faithful as a rock, the Father also sent to me. I know that he will do much work among the Gentiles, bringing them to the true faith. With God's help, he will cope with this task, and I think that perhaps the Father will send him somebody young to help. The Father always knows who to choose."

Jesus worried that he was not committing enough miracles to ensure that the High Priest Kiafa would wish to get rid of him. He was waiting for an opportunity to make a *great* miracle such that Kiafa would be so afraid of him that he would have no other choice but to kill him.

Some of the pilgrims suggested a more convenient way to get to Jerusalem and the group agreed to this shorter path. This meant that they would again pass through the village where Martha the sister of Mary Magdalene lived.

When they approached the village, they saw a group of women grieving; they were weeping and sprinkling their heads with ashes. The Apostles approached the group of women and Martha ran up to them in tears. Seeing Jesus, she said: "Holy man! My brother Lazarus died suddenly today. God bless his soul!"

Jesus felt that his hour had come. He would demonstrate to all the people that God had sent him. Only God was capable to do such a great miracle as resurrecting someone from the dead. Lazarus, the brother of Mary and Martha, was a sinless man worthy of such a miracle.

"Take me to him and I will try to help," Jesus said.

The women, continuing to weep and mourn, led Jesus to the house of Lazarus. At the entrance to the house there were people shaking their heads and crying.

Jesus said, "Please let me pass," and the people parted to let Jesus enter the house. Judas and the other apostles stayed at the entrance with the mourning residents of Lazarus' village.

"I am sorry about Lazarus," the rich tax collector said. "He always paid his tribute regularly."

"Do not rush to bury him," Judas said in response.

And, as if in response, out of the door came Lazarus, alive and healthy. He looked at the crowd and said: "Why is it that you are all gathered at my door?"

"You were dead," the tax collector said bluntly. "I myself came to you to see if you were indeed dead."

"God was pleased with Lazarus and let him live," said Jesus, as he came out of the house behind Lazarus. "God sent me to give life back to Lazarus."

"It's a miracle! A true miracle as we have never seen!" the people cried. "We believe in you, Jesus! You are the true Messiah! You raised Lazarus from the dead!"

"I would not have been able to revive him if it was not the will of the Lord, my Father. Who believes will be saved!"

The miracle of Lazarus being brought back to life spread quickly throughout the land of Judea. It was such an unprecedented miracle that many people came to believe in the divine origin of the carpenter's son from Nazareth in Galilee.

The news of the miracle quickly reached the ears of the High Priest and the Sanhedrin, and they were horrified. Now, not only Anna, the head of the Sanhedrin, but almost all of the council members wished to get rid of Jesus before he brought a great disaster on the unfortunate land of Judea.

Six
Jerusalem

JESUS AND HIS company approached Jerusalem. They could already see the houses of Bethany, the village that was only a two-hour walk from the gates of Jerusalem. Many pilgrims whose funds did not allow them to rent accommodation within the walls of Jerusalem stayed in this hospitable village.

Jesus and his companions belonged precisely to this poor group of pilgrims and they decided to stay in Bethany. From here, they would go to Jerusalem early in the morning, spend the whole day in the city, and then in the evening return to the village to sleep.

One problem was that there was a small mountain between Bethany and Jerusalem. It was called the

Mount of Olives because olive trees grew on its slopes. Olives, the fruit of these trees, had long been used for the manufacture of olive oil, which was highly appreciated not only in Judea but also throughout the East, and had been since the time of the pharaohs. The journey from Bethany to Jerusalem and back was arduous, but due to their poverty Jesus and his companions had no choice. They would spend the night in Bethany and then visit Jerusalem the next day.

Jesus called the two apostles Peter and John, and told them:

"My friends, you have to go to the neighboring village. There you will see tied to the fence a young donkey which no one has ever ridden. Untie the donkey and bring him here."

"The locals will not allow us to take their donkey," the apostles said.

"Tell those good people that a donkey is needed for the Lord, and they will not mind giving you the donkey."

The Apostles left, and the women began to cook dinner.

Jesus called Judas, saying: "My friend Judas. It is time for us to talk in the shade of an olive tree there on the hillside."

"I hear you, my teacher," replied Judas.

Jesus and Judas lay down under an olive tree away from the noise of the people who accompanied Jesus.

"Now the time has come when you and I must perform that which is intended of us." Jesus said softly. "I must pass through this ordeal before I can stand in front of my Heavenly Father; and you must perform the critical task that will cover your name with shame. Once again, I ask you, are you ready for such a challenge?"

"Master, I will do everything that the Lord requires of me," replied Judas. If God is planning to cover my name with shame, if this is necessary for Him, I will always be ready to do what He asks, and what will make God's plan successful. I will not spare my honest name for the works of God! I am willing to sacrifice it!"

"I always knew I could count on you," Jesus said quietly in a sad voice. "Let me explain to you the essence of the matter. My Father sent me to this earth because he loves his people. He created the first humans Adam and Eve. He loves his people, all people, not just the Jews, who are the chosen people. My Father wishes to open the way for humanity to experience the immortality of the soul. The obstacle to that is the sins of man, and the clearing of sins requires sacrifice. I do not mean those sacrificial animals that every orthodox Jew carries to the altar of the temple. They cannot atone for the sins of all humanity; the atonement for sins on this scale requires a special sacrifice. The Creator Himself must sacrifice what is most precious to Him, and I, His son, must be that sacrifice. Only bringing me to the altar of humanity can atone for the sins of all mankind. Do you understand?"

"Rabbi, it is an incredibly great sacrifice! It is awful to sacrifice one's own son!" exclaimed Judas. "Even I could not bear such a loss!"

Then Judas looked at Jesus with pain in his eyes. "And you, what will happen to you? How will it happen?"

"However hard it will be for me, I will bear it," Jesus said. It is necessary for the salvation of mankind."

"My teacher, let *me* replace you, please. I know how cruel the Roman legionnaires are. For them, the greatest pleasure is to watch the torture of poor victims. I do not want you to be subjected to their brutal punishment."

"It is my destiny; I was born only for this purpose. Your death will not atone for the sins of humanity," Jesus explained, "Your task is quite different. Be aware that we are engaged in the performance of the grand task that will be the salvation for all humanity. Any deviation from God's plan is not acceptable. Each of us has his destiny."

"What is my purpose, dear teacher?" Judas asked impatiently.

"The guards of Sanhedrin will not dare to arrest me when I am surrounded by the people. Kaifa will not allow them. He will be afraid of exciting the crowd because he does not want bloodshed caused by an uprising of the people. Therefore, he will want to grab me secretly. An arrest is impossible to keep secret in the daytime, and even at night it is difficult because my disciples always surround me. However, Kaifa must arrest me. So he will decide to arrest me at night, when there are fewer people around me.

The morning after the arrest, the people of the Sanhedrin will tell the crowd that I voluntarily left the city. Even if one of the apostles tells people that I was arrested, dozens of Pharisees will confirm that they saw me leaving the city. Many ordinary people will also confirm that I left the city because people will believe the Pharisees and accuse my apostles of being liars and troublemakers. All that matters is that the guards let me leave the city and then arrest me outside the city walls, waiting until people have dispersed for the night. So no one except my disciples will know about the arrest. Neither they nor we need the outrage of the crowd. It is not included in the plan of the Creator."

"And what is my role in all this?" Judas asked impatiently.

"I am coming to that," Jesus said softly. "So the guards have to arrest me at night, quickly and quietly. They would prefer that it happens on our way to Bethany, at the place where we would usually rest before we get to our overnight stay. In this place, only a few people will be around. For the guards, the problem will be that all people dress alike and in the dark they look alike. How will the guards recognize me and not confuse me with one of the other pilgrims? At night, this is an impossible task. They will need someone who can easily identify me, even at night, and point to me. In God's plan, he has entrusted you point to me."

"What? Send you to your death?" Judas eyes widened as terror seized him.

"Exactly, this is your task," Jesus said firmly. "It is not my will; it is what God asks of you. It is His will! Are you ready to fulfill the will of God?"

"The will of God? I have vowed always to do the will of the One who created the universe. How can I go against His will?" Judas said in a trembling voice. Only now did Judas realize what a terrible task Jesus was giving him. Judas had always hated informers with every fiber of his soul. Judas could feel that his whole body was covered in sweat and he felt a sharp pain in his chest.

Jesus continued: "Before my death, God does not want you to tell anyone of His plan and the fact that you are doing this according to His will. If you reveal this secret, there are those who can stop us, and our work will fail. This work, which God conceived for me, and for which He is sacrificing me, must not fail! Do you realize the responsibility of keeping the secret?"

"Yes, Teacher, I understand. I will not reveal this secret to anyone." Judas did not want his terrible task, but he could not break his word given to God. He would obey God's order and do God's will.

"Listen to the instructions for your task," Jesus continued. "You will go to Anna when I give you a signal. The guards will not want to let you see Anna. Tell them that you are on an important case concerning a preacher named Jesus of Nazareth. They will detain you and ask Anna what to do with you, and Anna will likely call you to him. Say to Anna that you are one of my disciples and that you are disillusioned by my teaching. Say that I have offended you and called you incompetent and greedy, and that you are tired of wandering around the country with me. Tell him that you are ready to point me out to the temple guards if they will pay you well for your assistance."

"But this is not true at all! Why would I ask for payment?" Judas asked.

"If you do not ask for payment, they will not believe you. I know their psychology. These people are greedy for money, and therefore they will be convinced that no one would help them without payment. So you have to ask for payment for your services. Only then will they believe that you are not deceiving them. To add to your credibility, you can say that you need money to buy a plot of land on which you are going to build a house and start a settled life. This will convince them that you are the same as them, that you have the same requirements of life as all those people with whom they are dealing. This way they will trust you more. In the evening, you will lead the guards to the place of our rest on the road and point me out to them. Your task ends with that, and you are then free to do whatever you decide to do. Do you understand your task?"

"Yes, I do," Judas said sadly. Judas was distraught; not because he knew that all humans on earth would blame him for the death of Jesus, but because he loved Jesus more than himself. He was terrified at the thought of Jesus being given over to the mercy of those pagan beasts.

"Do not be despondent, my friend," Jesus said to him. "You have been chosen by God to perform this task because of your loyalty and steadfastness. It is very important duty."

Judas looked into the eyes of Jesus. "I will do everything as you say, exactly as you have described," he said with a combination of determination and a terrible sadness.

Jesus looked at his faithful disciple and he explained to him the other truth that came with Judas' singular task. "In the coming struggle for the immortality of the human soul, you will have no more tasks because the rest of the apostles will not understand you what you did. They will not trust you and they will curse you. But do not despair because all of Heaven will know the truth. Remember that the apostles here on earth will never believe that you did this on the direct orders of the Lord. I hope that someday, there will be someone wise enough to understand that everything that happens on earth is subject to the will of God. But before that happens, the not-so-wise majority will not believe you, even if you tell them about the role of God in your actions."

"Now I know why people will curse my name forever," Judas said in despair. "It is hard to realize what I must give you into the hands of the beasts, but I will do as you have told me. I will follow the instructions of my teacher and his Father. I will never depart from the task that the Lord has entrusted me to do."

"I am sure of your loyalty," Jesus said.

"Oh my Lord, why do I have such a difficult task?" The words flew out of the mouth of Judas and he turned pale.

Jesus saw that the young man was in despair. Being himself in an agitated state, he understood the depth of Judas' feelings.

"Dear friend," Jesus said gently, "my Father created His plan for a great cause. He sacrificed his only son to carry out his grand plan, and you and I are parts of that plan. Do you think I can easily perform what is intended for me? I am horrified to think of the suffering that I will have to endure. To tell you the truth, I am afraid, terribly afraid! But I have no choice! I must fulfill my Father's will. Each of us is a victim. Each of us has a heavy mission, and we must perform our mission. It is our duty before God and our contribution to the future of humanity. Be strong my friend, you must do your duty!"

Jesus embraced Judas. Judas looked Jesus in the eye and said: "Teacher, perhaps, there is some other way."

"There is no other way! This is our destiny!" Jesus answered, and he wept.

"I would find it easier to endure the terrible suffering myself, than to give you to the Romans," said Judas. "I have seen in my hometown their awful cruelty."

Jesus overcame his weakness. "We must obey the will of the Father," he said. Do you understand this?"

"I will do as the Lord wishes," Judas said.

They slowly returned to the village. As Judas walked, he looked like a whipped dog. At the foot of the hill they met the apostles to whom Jesus had given the task of finding a donkey. They had with them a fine animal, and were urging him along with a stick.

Jesus looked upon the Apostles and said: "I will ride this young donkey to Jerusalem tomorrow. Feed him, please. When we go up to Mount Olive, you will help me to organize a solemn entry into the city. All the people in the city from young to old should be aware of my arrival. Is that clear to you, my friends?"

"The arrival of the king of Israel will be solemn," the apostles answered happily. "We will glorify everywhere all the miracles performed by thee, especially the revival of Lazarus! People should know about the arrival of the Messiah."

In Bethany a modest dinner had been prepared. After dinner, the apostles saw that Jesus had retreated with Judas to the hillside, and they envied Judas for being awarded such a high honor by their beloved Teacher. When Jesus and Judas returned, they looked at Judas with hostility

Jesus started a conversation: "My friends. I want to tell you that the hour when I must suffer, as has been destined for me, moves closer. It will be hard for you to remain faithful to me in these difficult days. The temple priests will not be satisfied just getting rid of *me*. They will require that my followers also stop preaching. I want to be sure that you will maintain your loyalty and continue to spread my teaching to as many people of all ethnic groups as possible. Your way will not be easy, but each of you must exert all your strength and talent to spread the faith and to teach everyone about the true and only God. That is your purpose in this world. Is that clear to you?"

"Yes it is clear," the apostles answered.

Although the apostles said that they understood, Jesus saw that they did not believe in the coming suffering of their Teacher. He saw that the apostles were convinced that a person who could work such wonders as the resurrection of a man from the dead would surely find a way to avoid the suffering of his own flesh. They did not know that his suffering would be a sacrifice in the name of all humanity, and that Jesus would not use the means at his disposal for his own salvation.

In the morning, they went to Jerusalem, and everything happened as Jesus had planned. At the top of the Mount of Olives, the disciples helped Jesus to sit on the back of the donkey on which they tentatively placed the attire of the apostles. Both the apostles and the pilgrims threw their clothes under the feet of the donkey and praised Jesus, shouting happily: "Glory to the Messiah! The King of Israel has arrived! Long live the Christ!" Their shouts and cheers attracted many people, some out of curiosity, and some out of a desire to touch the Saint in the hope that a particle of his grace would pass to them.

Accompanied by a crowd of enthusiastic admirers, Jesus entered the city of Jerusalem, heading to the Temple. The rumor of the arrival of the Messiah had spread throughout the city, and more and more people were coming to the Temple. It was just before the Passover holiday, when by ancient tradition every Jewish believer considered it his duty to come to Jerusalem with his family and perform the rite of sacrifice at the Temple. Not everyone could bring a sacrificial lamb, and those who could not bring a lamb with them hoped to purchase one in Jerusalem. The Priests of the temple had for a long time engaged in the trade of lambs. They bought lambs in bulk from major pastoralists and retailed them to those who wished to buy. The Priests were too lazy to trade outside the walls of the temple and they did the trading directly inside the Temple.

When Jesus, accompanied by the cheering crowd, entered the Temple, there was a brisk trade of sacrificial animals; the Temple had been turned into a market. For the Son of God, there was nothing more frustrating than seeing, with his own eyes, that sacred place turned into a muddy market where greedy Temple servants traded with customers. The feces of sheep dirtied the entire floor of the Temple and people trampled this muck everywhere.

In the heart of Jesus, the scene ignited outrage, and forgetting his honorable role of Messiah, he rushed to chase the traders from the Temple, shouting: "Get out of the Temple, vile merchants! How dare you turn the house of the Lord into a muddy, filthy market! The Temple is intended only to glorify and worship the Creator! Get out!"

Jesus did not rest until the last trader had left the Inner Temple. The people who had come to the Temple to pray watched Jesus' actions with approval. As for the Temple priests, they looked at Jesus with hatred in their eyes, but in the presence of the large crowd they were afraid to argue with Jesus. They helplessly clenched their fists, not daring to give the guards orders to arrest Jesus.

Jesus, having expelled the traders, began to read a sermon to the assembled people. The people were spellbound, listening to his every word and nodding their heads in agreement. Jesus carried on with his sermon, inspiring people to honor the Creator and fulfill all of His covenants. And he spoke of the life of the soul after the death of the flesh, and of the punishments that await sinners in the next life. He explained that God is kind and loves people; that God is willing to forgive their sins, and that every sinner who sincerely repents is entitled to the remission of his sins.

He did not explain that in order to have the ability to pardon sinners, God would offer a sacrifice to wash men of their sins. Why open to everybody, including the Temple priests, the secrets of the Father? The Priests would report the plan to Kiafa, and Kiafa, knowing about the sacrifice, would not ask for the death of Jesus.

Seven
The Last Supper

IN THE EVENING, when the worshipers in the temple had begun to disperse, Jesus and his disciples went to Bethany for the night. They walked with a large crowd of pilgrims and they passed the gates of Jerusalem without any problems. The apostles were very satisfied with the day and they enthusiastically discussed the events that had happened. Only Judas was thinking, and he was walking like a whipped dog, hunching his shoulders like an old man. Andrew was the first to notice.

"What happened to you, Judas?" he asked. "Aching back?"

"Leave me alone," Judas said sadly. "It's not my back. My soul hurts."

"Look, good people, our Judas has a soul!" Andrew tried to make a joke.

"Leave him alone; he is a whiner," Peter said. "Be happy! Rejoice that this day was spent in the service to God and our Teacher. Rejoice that the menacing guards decided not to chase us out of the Temple."

"I am disappointed that the guards did not attack us," said Simon the Zealot. "So there could have been a revolt against the hated Romans and the henpecked members of the Sanhedrin."

"Rebellion is not our goal," John said. "Our goal is to help our teacher with his preaching to reach the soul of every person."

"You're right, my brother," Andrew confirmed.

Judas in his mind approved the words of John, but his worry was about his task and the fate of Jesus.

They came to the Mount of Olives.

"We can relax now," Jesus said, pointing to a place near the old olive tree. "This is a convenient place to stay."

They lay down on the ground as the pilgrims continued their journey. Under the tree with Jesus there remained just a handful of people, and it was getting dark. Comfortably stretched out on the warm earth, Jesus said, "This is the place, Judas." Judas replied with a nod and silently stretched out next to Jesus. He was tired of his worries.

Their dinner awaited them in Bethany. The hospitable hosts had prepared not only dinner, but also a comfortable place with beds for Jesus and his disciples where they could have dinner lying conveniently after a hard day in Jerusalem. The dinner was modest: lentil soup, sweet peas and freshly baked bread. The host, Simon who was nicknamed Leper, apologized: "I'm sorry, good people, for a modest dinner. We could not afford to buy a lamb because all the pilgrims bought our sheep and the prices rose very high."

"Thank you, Simon. We are simple people and do not need expensive meals. We are happy with this what you have given us," Jesus said.

"There is a woman asking permission to see you. She says she wants to do you an honor," said Simon.

"Let her do so," Jesus said.

The woman entered, carrying a beautiful jar decorated with colorful paintings. She stopped at the bed of Jesus, bowing low and saying: "My heart feels that the beloved prophet needs a great honor. Let me anoint your body with expensive perfume—the pure oil of nard!"

Without waiting for an answer, she began pouring the precious oil from the jar on the head of Jesus, and she poured the oil until the jar was emptied, and then, with her hand, she began carefully rubbing the precious oil over the body of Jesus, saying: "Thank you, Jesus of Nazareth. Glory be to thee, a prophet and a healer."

John watched, and he thought: The host apologized to us because he could not afford to buy a sheep for dinner, and here is such profligacy. This oil is worth not less than three hundred denarii. For that kind of money, one could not only buy a sheep but also feed many hungry people who are in need of a piece of bread.

Looking accusingly at Jesus, John said to Peter: "I do not understand our teacher. Why did he allow this woman to pour the oil of nard all over him? We could feed many hungry people by selling this oil! In our impoverished country so many people go to bed without supper!"

"You're right!" said Thomas. "We teach the importance of charity and the unrighteousness of wealth, and this is a bad example to show the people!"

"You do not understand him," Judas said quietly. "How many times has Jesus explained to you… but to no avail."

"Judas, be quiet," Andrew said. "You're too young to talk about us. I also cannot understand our teacher; it is not a good example to give us."

Jesus listened to the disciples and said nothing until the woman bowed again and left the refectory room.

"You do not understand me," said Jesus patiently. You will always have the poor next to you: but you will not always have me. You will always be able to help the poor, and now is the time to say goodbye to me. In a short time, you will stop learning from me. Very soon the time will come and I will not be among you. A woman's heart is more sensitive. She has done what lay in her power; she was anointing my body for burial. In her heart, she felt that the hour was approaching."

The apostles listened to the words of Jesus in disbelief. What was he is speaking about? What kind of burial could this be? Jesus was young and in good health.

Only Judas was horrified when he heard those words from the mouth of Jesus. It meant that it was therefore time to fulfill what was intended for him. How painful it was to even think about it! It was easy for them, the other apostles.

They have no terrible problem in their soul, no special task that Jesus has entrusted to them, Judas said to himself. They think about the coming day happily, believing that it will follow the same pattern as today. Their ignorance allows them to be happy and careless.

Jesus said to his loved disciple Peter: "Listen to me, Peter. Tomorrow you will go to the city, and near the gate you will meet a man carrying a jar of water. You must go after him. See where he goes, and go there too. Meet the householder and give him this message: "The Master says: where is the room in which I may eat the Passover with my disciples?

"He will show you a large room upstairs that is all set up, and you can prepare for a celebration. There you will find everything you need to cook for the feast of the Passover, for Seder. Take any of my apostles with you to help with the preparation according to our ritual for this evening."

"I am listening to you, my teacher. All will be cooked as our customs and rules prescribe."

"I put my hopes in you. Now it is time for a rest. Tomorrow we will have a tough day."

Within an hour, the disciples had fallen asleep in the house of the hospitable Simon the Leper. Actually, Simon was not a leper; a permanent job with olives had dyed his hands so that he had very dark spots like a leper.

All the disciples slept peacefully except for Judas. Judas was not sleeping at all. Although he was the youngest of the apostles, he was the most familiar with the temple priests and their commitment to their caste privileges. Jesus had pushed the sellers of sacrificial animals out of the temple! They would not forgive Jesus for this. They would go to the Sanhedrin and seek punishment for Jesus. In addition, Judas was destined to help these stupid and greedy people grab his beloved teacher. How could he give them a defenseless Holy Jesus? And why had Jesus entrusted this task to him?

With pleasure, Judas would have switched places with Jesus in order to save his beloved teacher from the brutality of the Roman soldiers! But that was not what his teacher had decreed. Young Judas could not sleep all night. What a terrible situation! And there was no one he could complain to about his bitter fate. In addition, it was impossible *not* to do what was intended of him, what Jesus had asked him to do! The unfortunate Judas could not sleep even for a second.

Jesus also did not sleep well. He did not doubt the correctness of the path he was taking because he believed that his beloved Creator, his Father in Heaven, had inspired the plan. But he feared for himself. Would he be able to endure the torture and not disgrace himself? Jesus feared the weakness of spirit that is inherent in all people. He knew that the Roman soldiers were ruthless and didn't feel remorse, and that they exposed people to horrible tortures.

Thinking of the Romans, Jesus was sorry for those soldiers who were subjected to committing atrocities. Their souls would burn in hell forever. If it was malice or other such sins that moved them, then let their souls have that fate. But they would be tearing the flesh of Jesus out of ignorance, their own ignorance. If they knew and believed in the true God, the Heavenly Father, in the ethical standards that God has set for everybody, they would not torture people. However, faith had not reached them, and they did not yet believe in the Creator, the one God!

Jesus drew a deep breath. Pride filled his soul with the consciousness that his flesh would be sacrificed so that the belief in one God would triumph and so that the souls of men would gain the right to eternal life. For the sake of this great goal, he was ready to accept his punishment, however terrible it would be.

The day dawned sunny and clear. The apostles had breakfast and they felt ready for the upcoming day. They expected a joyful day and anticipated the celebration that evening would bring. It was the great holiday of Passover, the feast in honor of the liberation of the people of Israel from slavery in Egypt. Their release had been an act of God, who had sent his representative Moses to Egypt. Moses was not afraid of the almighty Pharaoh, and in the name of God he demanded the release of all the people of Israel from slavery. Pharaoh did not believe in the power of the Creator and dared to contradict Moses. God punished Pharaoh forcing him to free the people of Israel.

The upcoming Passover holiday inspired hope in the hearts of all the people of Israel for a speedy release from Roman oppression. Some apostles believed that it was just for this purpose that God had sent Jesus to the earth. They in their soul waited for when Jesus would reclaim their rights from the Romans and the governor Pontius Pilate.

They did not know that Jesus had another goal in mind. They repeatedly listened to the explanations of Jesus regarding the immortality of the human soul, but at heart they considered this secondary to the suffering of the chosen people under the Roman yoke. Only Judas believed to the very depths of his soul the words of Jesus, knowing that the teacher was sincere and that the purpose of his salvation was not only the people of Israel but all humanity. The Roman yoke was temporary because all empires are temporary. Assyria was once a mighty empire, but where was it now? Persia was also great and then vanished. And so it would be with Rome. A human soul is eternal, and it needs salvation. Jesus had a more important mission than the struggle with Rome. Only Judas knew about the goal of the Lord and of Jesus, his son.

All day the apostles prayed fervently, as was customary at this time of the year for all people who believed in the one God, Jehovah. Only Peter and John worked to arrange the festive dinner called Seder. They cooked everything that ritual required and they connected with the other apostles in prayer. The people gathered around, listening to the prayers of the holy men and repeating their words of prayer. In anticipation of a delicious dinner, priests sacrificed the last sheep on the altar, trying to free themselves from the rather boring procedure.

The day passed quietly without incident. Even the guards of the temple, not mingling with the crowd, quietly watched the apostles praying. Throughout the city there was a pre-holiday mood, and no one wanted to make a fuss. By evening, the crowd began to leave the temple, and Jesus signaled that it was time for their evening dinner. The guards followed Jesus and his disciples as they departed from the temple.

The room was all prepared for the dinner and the whole group settled on the beds. John wanted to lie down next to Jesus, but the teacher suggested that this place was for Judas. John was genuinely upset, as he considered himself the most beloved of all the disciples of Jesus.

"With what has this young Judean bewitched our teacher?" John asked himself. "Am I worse than this greenhorn? He could never preach persuasively. How will be he able to lead people if he is tongue-tied?"

Nobody noticed John's resentment and Judas did not pay any attention. Judas had no pride regarding his place of honor at the dinner; he was not thinking of pride. He continued to worry, dreading the approach of the hour when he was destined to fulfill his duty to Jesus. His agitation was understandable, and Jesus had placed Judas beside him to help Judas relieve the stress of waiting and prepare for the necessary accomplishment.

All the apostles of Jesus noticed his special relationship with Judas, and they were envious. They did not express their feelings in the presence of the Master, but they were full of suspicion and hostility toward an apparent pet and this embarrassed each of the apostles. They were embarrassed because those feelings were sinful, and contrary to the teachings of Jesus. The disciples knew this, but they could not overcome their negative feelings.

It was a ritual dinner, and according to this ritual, Jesus asked questions of the youngest in the room. Judas answered as best he could. Prayers required reading a prayer this evening, read in turn, and chorus. Scattered Judas answers supplemented by discontent of apostles with young Judas. Only Jesus gently and persistently continued to ask questions, as was the ritual.

Jesus broke the matzo and gave it to his disciples, saying: "I will not drink of the wine ritual today, because the hour is coming when one of you will give me into the hands of the guards, and thus will begin the hour of my suffering. I am sorry for the one who will give me. I am going to my designated path, in the name of a great purpose."

The disciples were surprised by the words of the teacher, wondering who would betray the teacher and point him out to the temple guards. They did not believe their teacher, and they continued to worry only about who was the closest to Jesus and who should be considered as such.

This upset Jesus. He saw that the disciples were not serious and did not think about the coming events.

They should be thinking at this hour about their mission and about which way to go after the death of Jesus. But the disciples did not believe in the imminent death of their teacher; they just thought about his greatness.

Jesus looked at Judas. Judas had calmed down a bit. He did not react on Jesus words that grief soon come to apostles. Judas believed that his grief already covered him with wing of need.

Jesus bent down to Judas and whispered in his ear: "The hour has come! Go. Accomplish what you intend to do."

These words pierced the heart of Judas as if they were a lightning bolt. Now all of his strength and all of his thoughts were directed to completing the task given to him by the Master.

Judas got up and walked out of the refectory. None of the apostles paid attention to his departure. Dinner was a long, drawn-out affair and many would leave the dining hall to look after their natural needs. But unlike the others, it was not because of the call of nature that Judas left the refectory. Instead, he hurried to the house of Anna to show the guards where Jesus and his disciples would rest on the way to Bethany.

Eight
Fulfillment of Destiny

JUDAS RAN THROUGH the dark streets of Jerusalem, hastening to lead the guards in time to arrest Jesus at the designated place. The People of Sanhedrin stopped Judas at the gates of the house of the High Priest Anna.

"Look who we stopped. It's one from the inner circle of that holy man who dispersed the traders in the temple," one of them said.

"Yes, I'm one of them. I hasten to see Anna, the venerable head of the Sanhedrin. Take me to him!"

"You want to see Anna? Are you going to kill him? Search him, Moshe!"

Moshe was a huge fellow with a black beard and was clearly one of the Sanhedrin guards. The biggest and most powerful men from all Judea were chosen to serve in the Sanhedrin guards. Moshe came to Judas. One hand gripped the throat of the young man and the other searched his clothes. Not finding any weapons, he released the throat of the unfortunate Judas, and said: "He does not have anything. What to do with him?"

"Hit him in the stomach and chase him away."

Moshe instantly fulfilled the first part of the instructions with such force that Judas' eyes popped from the pain. Panting, Judas shouted: "I came to inform Anna where it is easiest to grab Jesus of Nazareth. Let me see Anna!

"Not enough for him? Give him more, Moshe."

Moshe struck Judah's head with force, saying to his friends: "Maybe we need to ask the authorities what to do?"

"You're right, Moshe," one of the guards said. "It is easy to chase him away, but would our superiors praise us for it? Maybe the superiors will order that we seize the Prophet himself. Then this guy could come in handy."

"You think so?" the one who first gave instructions to Moshe asked. "Mordecai, go to the house and ask what to do with this freak."

Moshe continued to hold Judas so tightly by his arm that the blood in his arm stopped.

Mordecai returned from the house and said: "They told me to bring him in. Take him, Moshe."

Judas went into the house, followed by Moshe. In the house, a richly dressed urbanite was licking his lips and enjoying the remnants of the festive table.

"Do you know this beggar prophet?" he asked Judas.

"He's one of his inner circle," Moshe said. "I remember all of them and I saw him in the temple."

"Do you want to help us?" The chief asked.

"It is the reason I came," Judas said firmly. After the beating, his soul had grown stronger, and now he had no hesitation about performing his task. He was sure that he was executing God's will.

"Let's go to Anna. Tell him your terms."

They led Judas into the inner chambers of the house. It was a dark room, but Judas could see the high chair and a man sitting there, as if on a throne.

"Can you point us to your teacher?" Anna asked in a hoarse voice.

"Yes, oh venerable Anna," Judas said.

"Why do you want to pass him to us?" Anna said.

"I am tired of him wandering through the world without shelter and without hope for the future," Judas said, as Jesus had taught him. "I want to buy a piece of land and build a house for myself."

"This is commendable," Anna said. "Do not try to fool us! And do not think to point at some obscure person instead of your teacher. Our hands are strong."

"I am not such a man. I want to marry and my dream is to have a family. I need money for this and also peace with the authorities. I cannot deceive you; it would be prevent me from realizing my dreams."

"Reasonable. Enmity with authority is dangerous. How would you point us to him?"

"The teacher is a poor man. He cannot rent an apartment in the city for himself and for all of us, his disciples. He spends the night in Bethany. It is a long walk through the Mount of Olives from the city to Bethany. On the way to the village, on the outskirts of the mountain, the teacher usually stops to rest and to regain his strength. In that place, I will point you to Jesus of Nazareth, the preacher."

"Reasonable. How many people will be around him?" Anna asked.

"The Pilgrims probably left the city early today to get to the Seder. I think almost no one except his disciples will be with him."

"Well," Anna said, "Whatever your name is, know that we do not forgive cheating. We will take off your skin if you fool us."

"My name is Judas Iscariot, and I know very well what your guards are capable of."

"Lead the guards to this place of rest on the road," Anna said, pulling from his pocket a bag of money and throwing it toward Judas.

Judas deftly caught the bag and carefully hid it inside his clothes, saying: "I will not point a finger at Jesus. When we come to the place where the group is taking rest, the one whom I kiss will be Jesus."

"I do not care how you point the guard to your Jesus," Anna said. "And it is important that this dirty robber is in our hands without noise."

Judas remembered that this was exactly what Jesus had said to him: "They will want to get their hands on me without any noise." The teacher was always right. Truly He was fulfilling the will of his Father!

They left the private apartments of Anna and stood in the hallway.

"How many people will be with thy prophet?" the Chief of guards asked.

"With Jesus, twelve men, besides women," Judas answered.

"I need at least twenty guards," ordered the Chief. Turning to Moshe he added, "Now call everyone to come, and I will choose the best ones."

It took more than half an hour for the guards to come. Judas was worried that, moving at such a slow pace, they would miss Jesus; and at the appointed place they would find neither Jesus nor his disciples.

Now all Judas' attention was directed toward the successful completion of his mission. He could not fail Jesus and arrive too late. God's will must be done!

The security chief selected twenty of his strongest guards, and leaving his assistant to guard the house of Anna and the houses of the other officials, he followed Judas toward the gate of the city and the Mount of Olives. As Judas hurried, he was filled with anxiety.

The lack of Judas in the group celebrating Passover was noticed only when dinner was over and the group was leaving to spend the night in Bethany. To some of the apostles it seemed suspicious, and a sense of danger seized them. Silently and at a fast pace they left the territory of the city, calming down only when the gates of the city were behind them.

All the while Jesus thought about the impending pain and he could not suppress a feeling of fear.

It was completely dark when they arrived at their destination and they were eager to lie down and rest. Some belated pilgrims passed them on their way to suburban villages.

"Pray, my friends, so as not to fall into temptation," Jesus said. "I will pray separately from you."

Jesus began to pray to his Father: "Father, pass this cup from me! Help your son! Help me, please! I am afraid, but my will is always to obey your command."

And it seemed to Jesus that an angel came down from heaven and strengthened his spirit. He continued to pray and he prayed so fervently that all his body was covered in sweat; and it seemed to him, in the dark of the night, that it was not sweat, but drops of his blood running down his body.

After finishing his prayer, Jesus returned to the apostles. Tired and soothed by prayer, the apostles slept peacefully on the ground.

Jesus woke them up and told them to continue their prayer. Then he said:

"Before the first cock crows, you, Peter, will disown me, and not once."

Peter wanted to protest, but there was no time. He saw twenty figures hurriedly approaching them, all swathed in dark clothes. To Peter they seemed like black clouds in a hurricane, and he immediately sensed that something was wrong. He wanted to get up and run, but he could not. And fear fell not only on him, but on all the apostles.

One of the twenty figures, the one who was walking in front, approached the apostles, and seeing Jesus, rushed to hug and kiss the Teacher. Then the man who had been walking behind Judas rudely pushed Judas away from Jesus and grabbed the teacher with his strong hands. The disciples did not have time to recover before Moshe, the guard, quickly pushed Jesus toward his assistants, and they just as quickly led Jesus away from the frightened and bewildered apostles.

Judas slowly followed the guards. He was devastated mentally and physically. He walked slowly, not knowing what to do with himself. He had fulfilled that which Jesus had instructed him to do, but what to do next, he did not know.

He returned to Anna's house, but there he was told that Jesus had been taken to the High Priest Kiafa's house, where all the Sanhedrin were gathered to judge Jesus before morning. In addition, all the chief priests and the elders of the Jewish communities would come to the court. Their task was to determine Jesus' guilt and to pass him to the Roman governor for approval of his sentence and for punishment as a criminal.

As Judas was departing from the house of Anna, he saw that Peter was also there to inquire about Jesus. One woman asked Peter: "Are you one of those people close to this prophet? Something about your face is familiar."

Peter was afraid that she would expose him, and he hastened to answer: "No, you are mistaken. Judas remembered that Jesus had predicted Peter's denial of his teacher.

However, Judas had done what Jesus had told him, and he had performed mindlessly, as an obedient child follows the instructions of his father, not thinking about the consequences. Now was the time to think.

Judas reminded himself of the legend of Abraham, ready of his own free will to sacrifice his son Isaac to prove his love to the Lord. What happened then? The Lord, convinced of Abraham's loyalty to Him, did not allow infanticide.

So would He now allow the execution of Jesus, His son? Was Jesus worse than Isaac? Was he not a child to his father?

Judas' heart longed for the great miracle. He believed that at the last minute the Lord would send an angel down to earth and save Jesus from his cruel punishment. How else could it be? For the Lord who is kind to all people would surely rescue his beloved son from the clutches of the Roman monster.

These thoughts briefly calmed the soul of Judas, but only for a short time. Soon doubt, inherent in every thinking person, overpowered the mind of Judas again. Judas remembered the teacher's explanation about the necessity of this sacrifice. If the Lord intervened and sent an angel to rescue Jesus, then no sacrifice for the good of humanity would occur. If there was no sacrifice, there would be no salvation of human souls, and the whole plan of God would collapse. Jesus had been confident that he would be sacrificed; he would not allow rescue options. The Lord would not send an angel. There was not going to be a miracle!

Struggling with his emotions, Judas walked and walked around the city all night and all day, forgetting to rest or to eat. Although the apostles later claimed that Judas went to the premises of the court, where the members of the Sanhedrin decided the fate of Jesus, they were wrong. Judas did not go to court. Nor was he in the house of the procurator Pontius Pilate when they finally decided the fate of Jesus. Only those who hated Jesus and his teachings went to that place.

Even those members of the Sanhedrin who spoke at the meeting in favor of Jesus— and there were such people—were not admitted to the house of the procurator. Anna ensured that only those who supported his proposal to execute Jesus were allowed to attend; he did not want any risk. If even one of the representatives of the local people raised the question of pardoning Jesus, it was impossible to predict what decision Pontius Pilate would make. This patrician considered himself an educated man and he might decide that the innocuous preacher posed no danger to Rome. Anna himself knew that Jesus alone was harmless, but in the explosive environment of Judea, fire could occur from the flame of Jesus' speeches. Anna was not willing to take that risk.

Kiafa persuaded Pilate that there was an urgent need to carry out the execution quietly and to allow few people access to the place of execution. And there should be no announcement of the upcoming penalty. The less people knew about the death of Jesus and the other criminals, the calmer the atmosphere in the city would be. Let the people peacefully celebrate Passover; there was no need to excite them over such a commonplace event as the execution of criminals. Pontius agreed with the recommendation of the High Priest and ordered that at the time of the execution, an additional detachment of troops would be there under the pretext of maintaining order in the holiday period.

Judas noticed that Roman soldiers were appearing in large numbers on the city streets. He remembered the excitement in the city over the procurator's venture to build a water supply system; he, Judas, had been badly beaten by the Romans then. So Judas tried to get away from the streets where the soldiers were gathered. He walked along a different route, and at one city corner he saw a group of citizens traveling in the direction of the hill known as Golgotha. Judas joined them because he just wanted to be one of many.

But the Roman legionaries blocked the road and wouldn't let the people pass. Nor would they let the people go. Judas wanted to leave the crowd, but the Romans would not let him.

It wasn't until evening that the soldiers let people climb to Golgotha. To his horror, Judas saw on the hilltop three large wooden crosses, each with a crucified person bound to the cross. The sight was horrifying.

As if in a stupor, Judas moved closer to the crosses. Terrified, he recognized Jesus as one of the crucified. Jesus was unconscious. His head drooped, and his naked body was covered with bloody scars that were being invaded by wasps.

At the foot of his cross there were women crying. Among them, Judas recognized Mary, the mother of Jesus, and Mary Magdalene.

Suddenly Jesus opened his eyes and his eyes met the eyes of Judas. Jesus, unable to speak, could barely blink an eye; his glance toward Jesus was a mix of approval and suffering.

Judas could not stand the sight. He trembled, clutched his head, and began to leave the crowd of onlookers who were watching the slow extinction of human life on the crosses. Judas vomited and his face was covered with sweat. He stumbled repeatedly as he walked, trying to quickly leave this terrible place.

Judas walked aimlessly. He thought about his role in the death of Jesus. He did not care about his reputation but he worried about the reputation of the people he represented. Judas came to the walls of the temple. He was so pathetic and horrible that the temple guards did not stop him from entering the temple.

Kiafa himself was conducting the festive service surrounded by important priests in ceremonial robes. Judas slipped through the crowd of ordinary worshipers to the center of the Temple and he faced Kiafa. Judas was as pale as milk with dark burning eyes as he glared into the eyes of the High Priest. His appearance was so awful that Kiafa interrupted his prayer in mid-sentence.

Judas, in a loud voice, proclaimed:

"What are you, unworthy ones, rejoicing about? What do you celebrate? Do you think that you have freed yourself from an opponent? You do not care about His suffering. You cannot imagine what kind of trouble you have brought on the heads of our poor people with this action! You do not care about our people; you think only of your own tranquility.

"I, Judas Iscariot, declare that you have stabbed in the back the entire nation of Judah. It will take years, centuries, millennia, for our people to be rid of the anguish to which you have condemned them today. You have sown in the soul of all the peoples of the world a grain of hatred toward the Jews. And those seeds will germinate and the fruits will be the suffering of all the people of Judea. Believers in Jesus will blame not just you alone, but all the Jews for the torture and death of the Son of God!

"Jesus knew his fate. He deliberately prepared all that has been manifested, and you easily succumbed to his bait. I came to you on his instructions, passionate about his idea. But what a fool I was! I believed him, that only *my* name would be consigned to eternal damnation on earth. I did not realize that it was not only my name that would be doomed to eternal shame. No, the hate would spread to all the people of Judah.

Over many centuries, people will blame the Jews for betraying Jesus! I understand now that God has chosen our people not for joy and pleasure, but for suffering! I succumbed to the charm of Jesus and betrayed the Jewish people for the sake of the salvation of the rest of humanity. I did not betray Him, but I betrayed our poor people! Our people are not guilty! It is your fault only! Your soul will burn in hell for this forever and ever! I hate you!"

Judas pulled from his pocket the bag with the thirty silver coins that Anna had given him. He threw the bag to the feet of Kiafa with the words:

"Here are your stinking pieces of silver. Not for them did I do what I did. I carried out the will of Jesus, and I curse you!"

After these words, Judas turned and quickly left the temple and those who were partaking in the service there. Judas had to hurry; he had not yet completed his earthly affairs.

Nine
Hello Eternity!

Judas went to the gate of the city by a roundabout route. In the streets were many Roman legionnaires, and Judas tried to circumvent the areas where they were posted. Not that he was afraid of them, but the mere sight of these ruthless and evil individuals induced in Judas the desire to shun them. Judas circled the city just before nightfall. Suddenly, all the soldiers disappeared from the streets, and Judas hurried toward the gate of the city. The road was deserted both within the city and outside the gates. Even the people who at this time were usually leaving the city for the night had disappeared. Judas did not think about the people. He was devastated by what had happened, and he hastened to Bethany, expecting that the apostles would be hiding there.

The apostles were gathered in Bethany where it was relatively safe. Like Judas, the eleven apostles were confused. They were worried for their own safety and they could not find an answer to the question that tormented them: Why had Judas betrayed their Teacher?

First Andrew decided to ask this question aloud: "Jesus' prediction came true. He took the punishment at the hands of the damned Romans. But why did Judas betray him?"

Bartholomew supported Andrew. "What was missing for Judas?" "He was the favorite disciple of Jesus. Jesus often honored him by with one-to-one conversation."

"I think that Judas got greedy!" Thomas said.

"Greedy or not greedy, this man is not worthy to be our friend. That is for sure," Peter said confidently.

John interrupted Peter. "What should we do without our teacher? Where should we go and what do we say to the people? Do we say that he was a teacher for us and now we do not have him? Do we want to continue his preaching? I think we do, but who will listen to our words, when the Messiah, sent to earth by the Creator, was brutally executed by the Romans? We will not find support from the people."

"Do not panic, John." Simon the Zealot said. "Now is the time to start calling the people together for revolt against Rome."

"Do you want to get us crucified!?" Jacob asked. "Our teacher did not say anything against Rome. Jesus taught us *not* to call the people to revolt. That was not what the teacher wanted us to do. So what is our role after his death?"

"I think we need to refuse to meet with the people for a while," Philip said. "Let the high priest's anger subside, and then we can again take up the sermon."

"No, we should not allow people to forget Jesus and his preaching," stated Peter. "We must now continue his work. I will lead you to the people, as Jesus led us."

"What do we *say* to the people?" asked John.

"We will tell people about the life of Christ," Peter said confidently. "We will call people to have faith in our teacher, Jesus the Christ!"

The arrival of women interrupted this conversation. Mary, the mother of Jesus, was in such bad condition that the other women needed urgently to put her to bed. Someone brought a milk in a clay vessel gave it to the weeping Mary to drink.

In the room of men, there was silence. The apostles were silent out of respect to the mother of their teacher.

"May I? A female voice asked from behind the curtain that separated the females from the males.

"Come, Maria," Peter said, recognizing the voice of Mary Magdalene. "We buried him temporarily in the family crypt. In the morning, I will go and see how to wrap the body of my dear Jesus."

Maria sat on the spot where only a few days ago Jesus had taken food. She was deeply sad and thoughtful. The apostles waited for the details of the execution from Maria. None of them, for fear of being identified by the enemies of Jesus, had gone to watch the execution. But the women were not afraid and they had gone. They were weeping at the cross when Jesus, in terrible agony, ended his earthly life.

But Mary Magdalene did not want to remember the suffering of Jesus, and she was stubbornly silent. It was simply too painful for her to talk about the death of Jesus.

The apostles were still preoccupied with the question of what they should be doing now that Jesus was no longer with them. It seemed doubtful that people would listen to the disciples of Jesus, given the inglorious fate of their teacher. Would people be interested in the story of the life of a prophet who was unable to help people free themselves from the yoke of the heartless Romans?

Thomas was the first to raise the question: "What can I say to people if they ask how it happened that the almighty Lord did not defend his Son?" Thomas asked.

The question angered Mary Magdalene. "You did not listen to your Teacher!" she admonished. "How many times did He tell you that his task was not to fight against the authorities, but to save the souls of mankind. You need to explain to everyone that Jesus suffered to save his soul from eternal burning in hell. Is not that what my Jesus taught you?"

"Yes!" Peter said. "You're right, Mary! Jesus taught us that. As a senior in our community, I praise you."

"Since when did *you* become a senior in our community?" Mary asked in surprise. "Who can trust your seniority? You, who thrice refused Jesus. No, you cannot be a senior."

The words of Mary, a woman no less, outraged Peter. His face tightened and he was ready to create a dispute about his seniority, but just then the door opened and the voice of Judas came from behind the curtain: "This is me!"

Judas hurriedly entered the room, carrying a box with the community's money. He looked terrible. His clothes were soiled, and it appeared that he had spent time not in the city but in the barn with the sheep. His hair protruded from his head in all directions, and his eyes were bloodshot.

Judas threw the box on the table. "Here is what you have," Judas said. "Here is exactly a hundred and two silver coins and thirty seven coppers. I did not take a single coin."

"Where are those thirty that Kiafa gave you?" Peter asked angrily.

"I threw them on the floor of the Temple. I am certain you would not want to use the money paid out for Jesus!"

"You sneaky scammer! How dare you come to us here?" shouted John. "Did you bring the temple guards with you?"

Judas did not pay attention to John's angry shouting. With regret, he looked at the apostles; and with a calm and firm voice that did not match his terrible appearance, he said: "Jesus warned me that people on earth would not understand my actions. You do not believe me and I will not make excuses in front of you. I performed what was intended of me.

"Now that I have fulfilled my duty, I am ready to meet the Heavenly Court with a clear conscience! I do not care about your judgment. I will report only to the Lord! Jesus asked me to remind you that his execution was not in vain. His Father conceived it, all with the aim of offering his Son as a sacrifice for the salvation of the souls of men—to ensure the right of everyone to the eternal bliss of the soul.

"Who believes will be saved! Do not forget it! This gives you the mighty weapon to convince all people to believe in the Creator, which is God! Everyone is destined to fulfill his mission. Your mission is to bring all people to a belief in the Creator, regardless of their language or ethnic origin. Each of you will educate preachers, whose mission is to continue to attract people to faith in our Lord. And every preacher educated by you should in turn foster a preacher who will replace him. As long as there are people on the Earth who have not heard about the Creator, this must continue. Remember that who believes will be saved! Bring people to the faith! It is your destiny! I am leaving you in the hope that you will do your duty as faithfully as I have done mine. Goodbye!"

Having said these words, Judas turned abruptly and left the room. Those of the apostles who were thirsting to beat Judas did not even manage to get up from their seats as Judas disappeared.

Gone, leaving the entire community in disbelief! Judas, the one who had betrayed Jesus, reminded them of their duty, their purpose in life! And he said it as if Jesus himself had asked him. Even the tone of his instructions sounded like Jesus.

Mary Magdalene was the first to speak. "It seems that he told the truth. Jesus himself told me something very similar. "

"That bastard! How dare he teach us!" cried Simon the Zealot. "He, the traitor who betrayed Jesus!"

"I don't believe that he did *not* take money out of the box," John said.

"Count it!" Peter said in a commanding voice.

John obediently began to count the money. Judas had not lied. All the money of the community was in place. This amazed everyone.

A host entered the room where the apostles were assembled.

"Have you heard what Judas did in the temple?" he asked.

"What?" The apostles asked in chorus.

"He burst into the Temple, his appearance so terrible that even the security guards did not dare to stop him. He stopped the service and shouted at the High Priest and the other priests, lecturing them about their betrayal of the people of Judah. He threw on the floor the bag that contained the money that the High Priest himself had given him for pointing at Jesus. Then he fled. Kiafa ordered that the money be spent to buy a plot of land for the burial of the dead. He said: "If this fool does not want to take this money, then we will spend it for the benefit of the community."

"I cannot understand this Judas," Thomas said. "He was always so thrifty. Why did he refuse the money? It does not seem like him!"

"You all do not understand him!" Mary Magdalene replied. "He gave you money because you need money, and he does not need money in heaven. He told you that he had fulfilled his destiny. That means that his earthly business is over. Do not rush to judge the one whom you do not understand."

"What do you understand, woman?" Peter retorted. "Judas betrayed our Jesus out of greed, and then he changed his mind because his conscience devoured him. It happens. It was not for nothing that he spent so long in our society! Where was his conscience when he kissed Jesus there on Mount Olive? He led the guards to Jesus! We all saw it. No pardon for him!"

"No mercy!" The Apostles shouted in one voice.

"I repeat in the name of my beloved Jesus, do not judge him," said Mary Magdalene. Condemning Judas, you bring the sin of hatred to your souls. "It is unworthy of the Apostles. You must be pure from sin if you want people to listen to you."

"Do not listen to a woman!" Peter cried. "Judas betrayed Christ. His name shall be covered with shame forever!"

Judas did not hear these disputes. He had already heard from Jesus the fate of his name among the people on the earth. At this moment Judas cared more about the fate of the Jewish people! He was afraid that he, with his new reputation as a traitor, and the Temple priests thirsting for the death of Jesus, had brought suffering to the Jewish people for centuries to come. Those who believed in Jesus Christ would always identify the act of Judas and the priests with all the people of Judah, as long as the teachings of Jesus existed. Could it lead to the hatred and persecution of the Jews? Judas felt that as more and more representatives of different ethnicities believed in a new religious movement, increasingly the enemies of the Jewish people would circle. And this feud would be in the depths of Christians' souls; Christians would blame all the people of Judah for the misdemeanor of the ruling elite.

How could he not know this before? Why had he not discussed this with Jesus? They might have come up with another idea, such that all the guilt would be his alone, such that no one could extend the blame to the whole nation. Judas blamed himself, finding no justification for his stupidity.

For more than two days Judas could not sleep. His terrible worry about the fate of the people of Judah drove him forward into the unknown. He had no confidence in his purity before God. He did not see it as an excuse that he had been stupid and mindlessly followed the instructions given by Jesus. He was innocent before Jesus, but before the people of Judah, he felt that he was very guilty. Would the Lord forgive him for such a terrible crime against his chosen people?

He knew that when it came time to urge the Romans toward faith in the Creator and in his Son who suffered for the salvation of mankind, Peter or another missionary would not blame the Roman soldiers and

Pontius Pilate for the death of Christ. How would the apostles be able to convince the Romans to believe in Jesus Christ and at the same time accuse them of barbarism and cruelty to the Holy Jesus?

No, thought Judas, the missionaries would accuse *him*, and with him the entirety of the Jewish people. They would declare the Jews and their High priest guilty of the martyrdom of Christ on the cross! There was no justice on earth! How had Judas not understood this before?

Judas ran into the mountains without looking at the road. He was worried not for himself, but for his people. Due to his agony, poor Judas' soul pulled away from his chest and his voice broke the night silence of the mountain. He pleaded with God, asking the Almighty to forgive the betrayal and mitigate the fate of the Jewish people. He stumbled and fell, rose again, and ran and ran without caring where he was going. As he fled, he could think only of the terror of his act.

The road led to a plateau on the top of the mountain, and on the plateau was a lone tall tree. Judas could not see the tree, and as he ran, he banged his head against the tree trunk. As he fell, blood spurted from the wound on his forehead and flooded his face, making him blind.

Judas got up with difficulty and coming around the tree he continued to move forward. He reached the edge of the plateau, and blinded by the blood that filled his eyes, he stepped into the abyss. He flew, continuing to pray for God's mercy toward his people.

Judas fell on the ragged edge of a rock at the bottom of the cliff. A sharp pain shot through his body and his soul ascended to God, leaving his mortal body at the bottom of the rocky gorge.

About the Author

Viktor Shel was born in Odessa, the USSR. He immigrated to the USA in 1980 and from 1998 settled in city of Dublin, California. He began writing in 1998 using his native Russian language. Viktor's writing based on his experience in Soviet Union and USA. Being the immigrant from the Soviet Union, he dedicated his short stories to the lives of Jewish people from the Soviet Union in their former homeland and in the USA. In year 2005, his short stories were published in the emigre newspaper "East – West" distributed in San Francisco, Denver and Toronto.

In year of 2007, collection of these stories came out in the Canadian publishing company Trafford

Publishing as a Russian language book. At the same time, the same publishing house published the result of many years of hard work – novel "Оксана" (*Oksana*). The novel is an epic, describing history of a one family from 1941 until 1995.

In subsequent years, Viktor Shel published two more major works on the lives of his contemporaries – novel "Молочные реки" (*Milk River*), 2008 and the trilogy "Превратности судьбы" (*The Vicissitudes of Fate*), 2013.

Viktor Shel always had interested in history. His first historical novel "Лёвушка" (*Leo*) was written in 2008. It refers to events at the end of the nineteenth century in Russia, and described adventure of young Jewish boy who was kidnapped and managed run from kidnapers.

The historical novel "Острые клыки овец" (*The Sharp Fangs Sheep*) written in 2010 highlighted the adventures happened in the early sixteenth century. The young converts from Judaism escaped from persecution of the Spanish Inquisition and joined the Mediterranean corsairs in fighting with Spanish crown.

Currently, Viktor completed story in which the events happened in the first century AD.

In 2013, Viktor Shel translated the novel "Лёвушка" into English and published under the title "Young Leo".

Now Viktor dedicates all his time to translation of his works into English to make them available to English speaking readers.

LIST OF PUBLISHED WORKS

Детство Вилена (**Vilen Youth**), 2007
ISBN: 978-1-4251-2640-7

Оксана (**Oksana**), 2007
ISBN: 978-1-4251-5020-4

Молочные реки (**Milk Rivers**), 2009
ISBN: 978-1-4327-1876-3

Острые клыки овец (**Sharp Fangs of Sheep**), 2011
ISBN: 978-0-615-44692-9

ПРЕВРАТНОСТИ СУДЬБЫ
(**The Vicissitudes of Fate**)

Book 1 *Юность*, 2013
ISBN: 978-0-9890856-0-1
Book 2 *Зрелые годы*, 2013
ISBN: 978-0-9890856-1-8
Book 3 *Борьба за счастье*, 2013
ISBN: 978-0-9890856-2-5

Young Leo, 2013
ISBN: 978-0-9890856-3-2

Stories Told by an Old Jew, 2016
ISBN: 978-0-9890856-6-3

The Land of Milk and Honey, 2016
ISBN 978-0-9890856-7-0

www.ingramcontent.com/pod-product-compliance
Lightning Source LLC
Chambersburg PA
CBHW051051230426
43666CB00012B/2651